MASTER
SELF
PUBLISHING

(The Little Red Book)

2014 EDITION

Edited by Latasia D. Brown

Includes Index
ISBN 978-0-9886960-6-8

Library Of Congress Control Number: 2010918372

Printed in the United States of America

CONTENTS

Introduction

So, you've had an idea for a book you want to write but haven't done so because you think it'll cost too much or maybe it would be too difficult. What if I told you that there is a way to publish your book and make it available to millions with very little cost and without a great deal of difficulty?

As the Internet matured new opportunities arose and innovative minds dreamt up new ways of doing business. One of the industries that benefited from this was the publishing industry.

For the longest time the only way to become a published author was to find a publishing company who was willing to publish your book (in many cases with up-front fees) and in return you receive pennies on the dollar in royalties.

As a Self-Publisher you can avoid exorbitant upfront up-front financing to get your book published. You will not be at the mercy of a big name publisher. This new way of publishing allows you to become the publisher and determine the retail price of your book and how much you want to receive in royalties.

This book is written to provide you with a road map to becoming self-published. In this book you will find specific and detail step-by-step information you need to become successfully self-published. This includes instructions on how to obtain barcodes for the books; how to market the book to bookstores, public libraries and other retail outlets that sell books; and other tools you'll need to become a knowledgeable and successful self-publisher. This is the book I wish I had before I published my first book.

You know the saying...."everyone has a story to tell"....go forth and tell yours.

CHAPTER 1

WHAT IS SELF-PUBLISHING?

Self-Publishing is the method whereby the individual author becomes the publisher of record for his/her own work and utilizes a **Printer** to print the book and provide a mechanism whereby it can be offered for sale (such as on their online bookstore).

Becoming a Self-Publisher means you have to assume the traditional tasks of publishing that would normally be performed by the publishing companies. It means you have to obtain **Barcodes** for the books under the name of your publishing organization. You also have to perform the task of **marketing** the book to bookstores, public libraries and other retail outlet that sell books.

CHAPTER 2

WHAT WILL IT COST TO SELF-PUBLISH?

First let's look at what it would cost to use a traditional publisher. With a traditional publisher the author pays pre-press, marketing and promotion costs. The author may be asked to pay this cost upfront or have the publisher take it out of royalties earned. Either way the author will have to pay those costs. Those cost, can range from just a few thousand dollars to many thousands of dollars.

Many authors are deceived because Publishers offers advance payments. Advance payments range from $5,000 to $15,000 for the average author. An advance payment is based on a 1/3 of first print run total royalties. **But, you won't receive a royalty check until your advance is paid back in full.**

Also, the average royalties received from traditional printing is 5-15%.

With self-publishing the entry cost is low and you have greater control over your marketing cost. You pay your costs up front and whenever a book is sold you earn and keep the royalties. In self-publishing you get a greater percent of royalties (average 70%).

Here are some specific self-publishing costs. Some of these items are optional.

Item	Cost	Remarks
Create the book	$0.00	You can do this yourself
Editing	$0.00	Do it yourself or someone you know who can do it for free
Create Book Cover	$0.00	You can do this yourself
ISBN	$125.00	Cheaper if you buy more than one

Barcode	25.00	This is the barcode with the ISBN information on it
Trademark (Optional)	275.00	Trademark the book name. This is not a requirement to publish a book. This is optional.
Publish the book(Hard copy)	$35.00	If you use createspace.com
Publish the book (eBook)	$19.99	Get it on amazon.com, barnes&noble.com, apple iBookstore, Google, etc.
Get book reviewed (Optional)	$600.00	Kirkus alone cost $425. But, they are most important book reviewer to receive a positive review from. There are other reviewers that are far less expensive.
Marketing (Optional)	$1,370.00	Rely mostly on web based marketing tools which are inexpensive and provide greater returns. Utilize book expo's that reach tens of thousands of librarians and bookstores. Reach out to Distributors and use the IBPA cooperative marketing programs. These things will bring you the biggest bang for your buck.
Total	**$2,449.99**	

CHAPTER 3

GETTING STARTED

Determine the type of Book you want to write:

You can publish a book in countless genres depending on its theme and/or type. For example, fiction or non-fiction are two different types of books; and then there are books put into categories based on the theme of their content, like drama, mystery or history. Once you know what direction you plan on going in, it's time to determine some more details that will help organize your book into its finished product.

Determine the size of the book:

If the book is too large you may end up pricing it outside the reach of your intended audience. Larger books cost more to produce and hence, could cut into your royalties. Readers will buy books that are easy for them carry. Bookstores will carry books that fit into their limited shelf space.

Consider what the size of the book should be. The most popular standard sizes include:

- 8.5" x 11"   (standard catalog)
- 6" x 9" x 1.5 (standard novel)
- 6" x 4" (digest)
- 7" x 10" (text book)

The choice you make for a **Printer** will determine the size of the books you can publish. **Printers** only offer to print books in certain sizes.

Consider these when choosing the size of the book:
1. **Cost:** The larger the size of the book, the more Printers will charge to print it.
2. **Graphics Quality:** Larger size books allow more room for better graphics.

3. **Font Size:** What size fonts do you want to use. Larger size books allow for the use of larger fonts.
4. **Audience:** Books for older people and children are usually larger to allow for the use of larger fonts and graphics.

Determine the style of the book:

Books may be published as a **paperback** or **hardcover**. Hardcover is usually heavier and cost more to print. Hence, the retail cost for a book in hardcover is usually more than the paperback version. Some people consider the hardcover version to be too heavy for them to carry around, while others prefer hardcovers for their better quality paper and enduring quality.

Color or black & white:

You can print your book in color or black & white. Printing, in color cost more than black & white. Storybooks for children are usually done in color. Novels, text books, how-to books are normally done in black & white.

Develop a publishing timeline:

In the publishing industry everything is timing and timing is everything. Everywhere you want to place your book, like bookstores and libraries, operate on a timeline. In order to get your book into bookstores and libraries you must know and adhere to their timelines. For the most part, determine at the end of the year what they will carry on their shelves for the next year.

In order to enhance your chance of getting your book into bookstores and libraries you must get your book **reviewed**. Most libraries and bookstore will not consider buying your book without the appropriate reviews. Book reviews take a certain period of time depending on who is doing the review. See **Chapter 9** on Book Reviews for more details.

Here is an example of A Publishing Timeline:

Itinerary	When
Determine the type of book	Jan
Pick a Printer (POD)	Jan
Determine the size of the book	Jan
Determine the style	Jan
Determine color v. black & white	Jan
Write the book	Jan-Feb
Get the book edited	Feb
Obtain the barcode	Feb
Copyright the book	Mar
Submit manuscript for reviews (pre-published)	Mar
Obtain an LCCN/CIP	Mar
Publish the book	Apr
Get the book reviewed (post-publication)	Apr-Oct
Start marketing the book to bookstores, libraries, consumers	Oct

Write the book:
Research, gather the information and write the book. Before you start writing you should pick a Printer (or Print on Demand Company [POD]). PODs have their own template that you can download that will work with Microsoft Word or other applications you utilize. Writing your book with the template saves you a great deal of time and effort by allow you to format as you go.

Get The Book Edited:
You can become both the author and editor for the book. However, it is highly recommended that a different pair of eyes review and edit the book. They are likely to catch mistakes you miss and see the book from the perspective of your target audience. You can ask someone you know or you can obtain editing services from the PODs listed in **Chapter 8**. PODs provide this service for a fee. Other editing services can be found at:

Editors for Hire: *http://editorhire.com*
Edits Online: *http://www.editsonline.com*
The Word Process: *http://thewordprocess.com*

CHAPTER 4

OBTAIN THE ISBN/BARCODE

In order to sell your book in retail stores (online or in storefronts) you have to assign a **barcode** to your book. A barcode provides information on the book --such as the price -- and uniquely identifies that book as belonging to you and as being a different product/books. *Your book cannot be sold in stores without the barcode.* The information contained on the barcode is called the International Standard Book Number (ISBN).

You can buy an ISBN/barcode for your book by going to Bowker Identifier Services at: **www.myidentifiers.com**. When you buy the ISBN at the Bowker website they also offer you the opportunity to create a barcode with the ISBN for an additional fee.

An ISBN consists of a 13 digit code that can also be displayed as a 10 digit code that looks like this:

> ISBN 13: **9780615271811**
> ISBN 10: **0615271812**

A different ISBN is required for every different type of book. For example, the hardcover, paperback, audio version, and e-book versions must each have different ISBNs. A corrected copy of the book must also have a different ISBN.

The ISBN must also be displayed on the inside of the book on the **copyright page** (see example at Appendix A). You can buy a single ISBN or multiple ISBN's. Price ranges from $125 (for one), to $250 (for 10).

This is a sample image of a barcode with the ISBN information. This barcode must be displayed on the back of the book cover.

CHAPTER 5

COPYRIGHT THE BOOK

In order to obtain legal protective status for the content of the book you must copyright the book. Copyright gives you the ability to sue and obtain statutory damages from someone who infringes on your copyright.

In order to copyright the book you must register with the Library of Congress at **http://copyright.gov**. It is a simple process that takes only a few minutes.

Copyright can cost $35.00, and gives the author lifetime protection of his/her work. It can take up to six months for the registration process to be completed.

The contents to be copyrighted must be uploaded as a **PDF** file. You can buy a PDF converter at the sites below. You can also do a Google search for more choices.

Microsoft Office 2007 or 2010 - $0.00:
Allow you to save your document as a PDF document. Buy from any computer store.

Nitro Pro 7 - $99.00:
Convert to PDF and allow you to edit the document in PDF format. http://www.nitropdf.com

CHAPTER 6

OBTAIN A LIBRARY OF CONGRESS CONTROL NUMBER (LCCN)

A Library of Congress Catalog Control Number is a unique identification number that is assigned to the catalog record created for each book in its cataloged collections. Librarians and distributors worldwide use it to find your book and expedite processing. Some libraries will not carry a book that does not have an assigned LCCN.

You have to apply for the LCCN. Once you are assigned a number you have to place it on the copyright page of your book.

Eligibility: To be eligible for an LCCN the book publisher must be from the U.S. and list a U.S. place of publication on the title page or copyright page of their books.

Cost: There is no cost to obtain an LCCN.

Process: To get an LCCN you must first sign up for a PCN account. A Pre-assigned Control Number (PCN) is a Library of Congress Control Number that has been "pre-assigned" to a given work prior to the work's publication.

1. First, you must to sign up for a PCN account by submitting an Application to Participate. When the application has been approved, an account number and password will be sent to you via email. This process takes one to two weeks. Open an LCCN Account at: ***http://www.loc.gov/publish/pcn/*** (Click the *"Open an Account"* link then the *"Application to Participate"* link at the bottom of the page.
2. Then you have to logon to the PCN system and complete a Pre-assigned Control Number Application Form for each title for which a pre-assigned control number is requested.
3. Upon receiving the number, the publisher prints it on the copyright page in the following manner:

Library of Congress Control Number: 2007012345

4. Send a copy of all books for which a PCN was provided immediately upon publication. Failure to meet this obligation may result in suspension from the program. The book will be kept by the Library of Congress and will not be returned. Send a copy of the book using one of the following methods.

U.S. Postal Service:
Library of Congress
US & Publisher Liaison Division
Cataloging in Publication Program
101 Independence Avenue, S.E.
Washington, D.C. 20540-4283

Commercial Shipments:
Library of Congress
USPL/CIP 20540-4283
9140 East Hampton Drive
Capitol Heights, MD 20743

Cataloging for a book that is already published:
All works submitted to the Copyright Office to meet copyright obligations are also reviewed by Library of Congress selection librarians. Works selected for addition to the Library's collections are assigned a cataloging priority and cataloged according to that priority. Publishers should also consider working with a professional librarian at a local library to obtain cataloging. You can check the cataloging status at: (*http://catalog.loc.gov*).

CHAPTER 7

OBTAIN A CATALOGING IN PUBLICATION PROGRAM (CIP)

Catalog In Publication program (CIP) is a bibliographic record prepared by the Library of Congress for a book that has not yet been published. The bibliographic record is sent to the publisher, libraries, book dealers, and bibliographic networks worldwide.

The Library of Congress is no longer issuing both an LCCN and a CIP for the same publication. You may choose to obtain the LCCN or the CIP but not both.

Applying for CIP: Visit *http://www.loc.gov/publish/cip/* (Click the *"Open an Account"* link then the *"Application to Participate"* button at the bottom of the page.

1. First, complete the application to participate and obtain an account number and password. The account number and password provide access to the form for requesting CIP data. This process takes one to two weeks.
2. While completing the application process you will be asked to upload a copy of your document. WordPerfect and Microsoft Word files can be submitted as ".txt" files.
3. Upon completion, the CIP data will be emailed to you. The CIP data must be printed as provided on the verso of the copyright page following the legend:

Library of Congress Cataloging-in-Publication Data.

4. Submit a copy of the book to the CIP Division immediately upon publication.

The difference between the LCCN and CIP is that CIP bibliographic record is distributed to publisher, libraries, and book dealers, but LCCN is not.

The CIP program and PCN program are mutually exclusive. Titles processed in one program are not processed in the other program

For information visit the Library of Congress FAQ page:
http://www.loc.gov/publish/cip/faqs/

CHAPTER 8

PRINT THE BOOK

In order to self-publish you need the services of **Print On-Demand** companies, or PODs which are organizations that will print your book and make it available to distributors who purchase books on behalf of libraries and bookstores. Additionally, PODs offers services such as placing your book on Amazon.com, Barnes & Noble bookstore, Barnes&Noble.com, Borders bookstore, Borders.com and promote them to libraries and independent bookstores.

Printers allow you to publish your book with no or very low upfront cost. They also allow you to buy author copies of your book at very low rates and retain copyright ownership of your work.

Additionally, PODs offer templates for you to download and create your book. They offer you the opportunity to publish your book in different sizes. In addition to hard copy they offer you the opportunity to publish your book as an audio book or as an e-book.

If you do not want to become a distributor be sure to choose a POD that will make your book available to distributors.

Below is a list of some of the best POD's.

CREATESPACE:
https://www.createspace.com

Services:
- Custom cover design or create your own
- Full professional editing and text layout
- Make book available to distributors
- Make book available to online and offline retailers
- Make book available to libraries and academic institutions
- Personal marketing representative

- Retain all rights to your book
- Create an online bookstore
- Purchase author copies at very low price
- Placed on amazon.com

Pricing:

- There is no setup fee
- The only upfront cost is $35.00 if you chose to purchase the Extended Distribution Plan (which includes distribution services, listing on amazon.com and other marketing opportunities).
- Set your own retail price
- $0.85 to $6.65 per author copy of your book depending on the number of pages in the book
- Earn 80% Royalties from CreateSpace online store
- Earn 40% Royalties from distribution sales
- Earn 60% Royalties from Amazon.com

eBook:

- Createspace also has an ebook program with amazon.com that lets you quickly publish your book as an ebook on amazon.com. See the eBook Section (Chapter 14).

LIGHTNING SOURCE:
http://www.lightningsource.com

Services:

- Custom cover design or use your own
- Make book available to distributors such as Ingram Books, Barnes & Noble, Amazon.com, and others
- Retain all rights to your book
- Purchase author copies at very low price

Pricing:

- The only upfront cost is $12.00 per year.
- Set your retail price
- Set your wholesale discount

eBook:

- Lightning Source also offers ebook service. See Chapter 14 for more details.

LULU:
http://www.lulu.com

Services:
- Custom cover design or use your own
- Book printed in paper and e-book format
- Distribute to retailers and wholesalers
- Set your own Price
- Retain all copyrights
- Marketing services

Pricing:
- Use the calculator on the website to determine what it would cost to publish your book
- Set your retail price
- Set your wholesale discount

eBook:

    - Lulu also has an ebook program. See Chapter 14 to learn more about their ebook program.

CHAPTER 9

GET THE BOOK REVIEWED

Book reviews are key to promoting your book to libraries and bookstores. Many libraries and bookstores will not accept your book unless certain reviewers have analyzed it.

To get your book reviewed you have to solicit reviews from specific book reviewers. Some organizations charge a fee to review your book, while others do not. Some will only review works that have not been published yet, while others will review published works and unpublished works.

One of the advantages of having your book reviewed is that some review organizations will publish their review of your book on their websites and newspapers thereby publicizing your book to a wider audience.

Below is a list of review agencies and the information you need to solicit reviews from them.

Kirkus Indie Reviews:
http://www.kirkusreviews.com/indie/about/
Kirkus provides reviews to independent publishers. This is a very important review to have. A positive review will gain the attention of libraries and bookstores.

Cost: $425.00

Booklist:
http://www.booklistonline.com/GeneralInfo.aspx?id=65
Booklist reviews books for the American Library Association. They review up to 60,000 books annually. Publishers whose books were not selected for review will not be notified.

Cost: Free

Send copies to:

> Booklist
> American Library Association
> 50 E. Huron Street
> Chicago, IL 60611-2729

Whom to Address:

Adult Books: Brad Hooper, Adult Books Editor

Books for Youth (Children's and YA): Gillian Engberg: Managing Editor (Books for Youth).

Graphic Novels: Ian Chipman, Associate Editor

Media: Contact Sue-Ellen Beauregard, Media Editor (for special video, audio recording, and audio book procedures).

Reference Books: Contact Mary Ellen Quinn, Reference Books Bulletin Editor (for special reference books procedures).

Library Journal:
http://www.libraryjournal.com/csp/cms/sites/LJ/SubmitT oLJ/TitlesForReview.csp

The Library Journal generally focuses on pre-published books, but will review published books.

Cost: Free

Subscribe to the LJ Review Alert for status:
http://www.libraryjournal.com/csp/cms/sites/LJ/info/new sletterSubscription.csp

Include the following information: author, title; name, address, and telephone number of publisher; date of publication; price; number of pages; and ISBN and LC numbers if available. Please indicate whether any illustrations, an index, or bibliography will be

included; also include a brief description of the book, its intended audience, and information on the author's background.
Address materials to:

> Book Review Editor
> Library Journal
> 160 Varick Street, 11th Floor
> New York, New York 10013

AALBC (Black Issues Book Review):
http://www.aalbc.com/reviews/reviewer_guidlines.htm

The AALBC review books published by black authors. Reviews both pre-published and published books. Offer two types of reviews: *Commissioned Review* and *Book Review Consideration*. The review period is six weeks. The review will be posted on the AALBC website for one month.

Commissioned Review ($299):
Go to this link and follow the instructions for Commissioned Review.
http://www.aalbc.com/reviews/reviewer_guidlines.htm

Book Review Consideration (free):

Mail fiction titles to (if book is not available on Netgalley or Amazon):
AALBC.com
1325 5th Ave. Suite 2K
New York, NY 10029

Non-fiction   titles   only
First send an email with a description of your non-fiction title to ***kam@aalbc.com.***

They will review the information and decide whether or not to review the book. If they decide to review the book a mailing address will be provided at that time.

Get Books Reviewed:
http://www.getbookreviews.com/services.html

Get Books Reviewed reviews published and pre-published books. They offer two types of reviews: Rapid Review and List Your Book Available for Review.

Rapid Review ($150):
It takes two weeks to complete review. They post the review to online sites including but not limited to: Amazon.com, Barnes&Noble.com, PressMethod.com, I-Newswire and ClickPress.com.

List Your Book Available for Review ($25):
List your book for six months. Reviewers, editors, producers, talk show hosts and other industry professionals visit the site regularly looking for new books to review. Once someone decides to review your book you will be notified.

Independent Professional Book Reviewers
http://www.bookreviewers.org

Each review will be posted on Amazon, Barnes and Noble and other websites. Review works from established publishers and self-publishers.

Cost: $50-$90 for books with 200-400 pages.

To submit your book for review provide the following information and send it to: ***reviews@bookreviewers.org***.

1. Full name with valid e-mail address.
2. Postal address
3. Title of book
4. Category/genre
5. Format: Has it been printed or is it an E-book?
6. Number of pages
7. If you have a preference for a reviewer, give them their name; otherwise, they will assign a reviewer
8. Provide a brief summary of your book. (A short paragraph or a few lines)

IBPA Direct Mail Services ($210):
http://www.ibpa-online.org/programs/coopcats_bfr.aspx

Currently mailed quarterly (January, April, July, and October) to approximately 3,500 book reviewers at newspapers, magazines, websites, blogs, radio and television shows.

You must send the following:
1. A 300 DPI (high resolution) TIFF formatted file (in CMYK color) book cover approximately two (2") inches tall to *designer@IBPA-online.org*. Please indicate program and title in the subject heading. (If you are unable to send a digital file, mail the books front cover to IBPA as soon as possible).
2. Title, subtitle and author.
3. A 100-word description of the book
4. ISBN, price, number of pages, 1-3 wholesalers/distributors.
5. Book's suggested genre.
6. Publishing Company name and address.
7. Website or email address.

You can also get your book reviewed by major newspapers. They do not charge for book reviews, however, they will determine which books they want to review. Some do not accept unsolicited review request. **Appendix B** contains a list of contact information for the major newspapers. Visit their website to learn more about their review program.

CHAPTER 10

GET THE BOOK DISTRIBUTED

Distributors play a key role in getting your book into bookstores and libraries. When a bookstores or libraries want to stock a book on their shelves they turn to the book distributor to place their order. The book distributor in turn goes to the publisher or POD to obtain the book and deliver it to their clients (bookstores and libraries).

Distributors provide a one-stop shopping source for bookstores and libraries. Instead of a bookstore or library having to go to every publisher to purchase their book they go to the Distributor. This saves bookstores and libraries a great deal of time and resources. In return for providing this service the distributor charges a fee (20-30% net) which is taken out of the purchase price of the book. Hence, the author's royalty is reduced by the amount of the distributor's fee.

If you choose a POD that already has a relationship with distributors you do not have to establish your own relationship with a distributor.

When marketing to distributors you should do the following:
- send a copy of your book
- include information about who is providing sales, marketing and distribution services on your behalf
- include a marketing plan (if requested)
- provide a copy of your catalog (see **Appendix H**)
- include in the catalog:
  - how many books are in a cartoon
  - how many units were published
  - list book reviews

Some of the well-known distributors that most bookstores and libraries work with include the following:

Ingram Book Company:
http://www.ingrambook.com/default.aspxs.

Baker & Taylor:
http://www.btol.com

Atlas Books:
http://www.atlasbooks.com

Bella Distribution:
http://www.belladistribution.com

BCH Fulfillment Distribution:
http://www.bookch.com

Book Hub:
http://www.book-hub.com

Book Masters Distribution Services:
http://www.bookmastersdistribution.com

Books to Market Now:
http://www.bookstomarketnow.com

David Brown Book Company:
http://www.oxbowbooks.com

C&B Books Distribution:
http://www.cbbooksdistribution.com

Cardinal Publishers Group:
http://www.cardinalpub.com

Consortium Book Sales:
http://www.cbsd.com

Diamond Book Distributors:
http://www.diamondcomics.com

Greenleaf Book Group:
http://www.greenleafbookgroup.com

Independent Publishers Group:
http://www.ipgbook.com

National Book Network:
http://www.nbnbooks.com

ACCESS THE IBPA/INGRAM MARKETING PROGRAM:

This program lets you gain access to Ingram Books with less than 10 titles as a publisher. It lets you advertise to over 28,000 vendors listed in the Ingram database. This includes 10,000 book retailers, 14,000 librarians, and 4000 international accounts.

You must first be listed with Ingram Books. The fee for this listing is $300. It normally cost $950.

Once you are listed in Ingram Books you can advertise in the *INDEPENDENT VOICE, ADVANCE* Magazine and to Wholesalers and Distributors. Advertising cost $350 per magazine.

Start by visiting the IBPA website to learn more about program and how to sign up for it: ***https://www.ibpa-online.org/programs/ingramprogram.aspx***

CHAPTER 11

PLACE THE BOOK IN LIBRARIES

Libraries buy books to add to their catalog and make them available to the public. Hence, libraries are a key target audience to market your book to.

There are thousands of libraries at the national, state and local levels. Libraries include public libraries, K-12 libraries, college libraries, junior college & university libraries. Key things to do to get your book into libraries:

- make sure the book have a page of contents & index
- get a LCCN/CIP
- Utilize independent book publishers marketing programs targeted to libraries
- participate in book expos specifically targeted to librarians
- engage in direct mailing. promote the book using flyers (do not send a copy of the book)
- Utilize PODs marketing programs targeted to libraries
- get book reviews

LCCN/CIP:
Having a LCCN and/or CIP is also key to getting books placed in libraries. Having an LCCN or CIP saves the libraries the hassle of having to create a catalog data record for your book.

You can also chose to market directly to libraries. If you chose this route there are two ways you can market to libraries, Book Expos and Direct Mailing.

INDEPENDENT BOOK PUBLISHERS:
The best way to promote your book to libraries is through the **IBPA Direct Mail Library program**. The Program cost only $215 per mailing. To learn more about the program and register for the service visit the IBPA website at:

http://www.ibpa-online.org/programs/library.aspx

The Public Library program is currently mailed at the end of every month; the K-12 Library program is mailed quarterly (December, March, June and September deadlines) ; the College, Jr. College & University Library program is mailed quarterly (December, March, June and September deadlines).

A certain amount of fliers are needed for the public library mailing: 4,000 fliers are needed for the Public Library mailing, 4,000 for the K-12, 3,200 for the college and junior college & university library mailing. Flyers must be submitted to the mailing house within 10 days of the registration deadline. They are mailed out within 20-25 days after the deadline.

Flyers must be
- Unfolded 8-1/2" x 11" unfolded.
- Printed one- or two-sides
- Not to exceed 100# paperweight.

Information To Be Included On The Flyer/catalog:
1. Category for acquisition librarian
2. ISBN and price
3. Publishing company name & address
4. A list of major wholesalers/distributors that carry the title
5. If the book was reviewed, list that as well.

BOOK EXPOS:
There are a number of Book Expos that are held throughout the year and are heavily attended by librarians who are searching for new books to add to their inventory. The best two methods to get your book displayed at Book Expos are as follows.

IBPA
(*http://www.ibpa-online.org/pubresources/exhibits_PMA.aspx*)
IBPA is one of the organizations that can represent your book (for a small fee) at these book expos.

The Combined Book Exhibit
(*http://www.combinedbook.com/exhibit-schedule_8_2010.html*)
The Combined Book Exhibit is also one of the organizations that can represent your book for you at book expos.

You can also choose to represent your own work by paying a nominal fee and become a vendor at the expo.

Annual book expos include the following:

Name	Location	Month
2014 American Library Association Midwinter	Philadelphia, PA	24-27 Jan 2014
2014 Michigan Reading Association	Grand Rapids, MI	16-17 Mar 2014
2014 Public Library Association	Indianapolis, IN	12-14 Mar 2014
2014 The London Book Fair	London, UK	8-10 Apr 2014
2014 Texas Library Association	San Antonio, TX	8-11 Apr 2014
2014 Florida Library Association	Lake Buena Vista, FL	8-9 May 2014
2014 BookExpo America	New York, NY	29-31 May 2014
2014 New Jersey Library Association	Atlantic City, NJ	3-4 Jun 2014
2014 American Library Association Annual	Las Vegas, NV	27-30 Jun 2014
2014 Frankfurt International Book Fair	Frankfurt, Germany	9-13 Oct 2013
2014 New England Library Association	Boxborough, MA	19-21 Oct 2014
2014 New York Library Association	Saratoga Springs, NY	6-7 Nov 2014
2014 California Library Association	Oakland, CA	7-9 Nov 2014
2014 Pennsylvania Library Association	Lancaster, PA	29-30 Nov 2014
2014 Illinois Library Association	Springfield, IL	31 Dec 2014

DIRECT MAILING:

You can also choose to market directly to libraries. If you choose this route here is what you need to know. To engage in Direct Mailing you need flyers/catalog and a mailing list. You can see examples of flyers/catalog at **Appendix G.** Your flyer should include the following information:

- Image of the book
- A brief description of the book
- Intended audience
- Author
- Number of pages
- ISBN
- Publisher
- Publisher website
- Date of publication
- Retail price
- Retail location
- Distributors (at least two)
- Author background

To obtain a mailing list you can purchase it from a List Service or do a Google search and build your own list. In order to give you a head start I have provided you with a list of State libraries contacts at **Appendix C.**

CHAPTER 12

PLACE THE BOOK IN BOOKSTORES

In addition to the chain bookstores such as Barnes & Noble, Borders, Books-A-Million, etc., there are thousands of independent owned bookstores. Some of these stores cater to specific demographics and type of books while others cater to all demographics and types of books.

INDEPENDENT BOOKSTORES:

One of the best ways to market to these bookstores is through the IBPA's Direct Mail Cooperative Catalog program that targets independent bookstores. The cost is $230 per mailing. See details about the program at:

http://www.ibpa-online.org/programs/coopcats_bksllr.aspx

Catalogs are mailed on a quarterly basis to approximately 3,500 chain and independent booksellers across the U.S (January, April, July, and October).

You must provide the following information in the online registration form:
1. A 300 DPI (high resolution), TIFF formatted file (CMYK color) of book cover approximately two (2") inches tall to *designer@IBPA-online.org*. Please indicate program and title in the subject heading. (If you are unable to send a digital file, please mail the books front cover to IBPA as soon as possible).
2. Title, subtitle and author.
3. A 100-word description of your title.
4. ISBN, price, number of pages, a maximum of three wholesalers/distributors.
5. Book's suggested genre.
6. Company name and address.
7. Website or email address.

Independent bookstores represent an enormous opportunity to sell books. There are thousands of these bookstores scattered throughout the country. These are bookstores with one or multiple locations. They are usually family-owned. They are always on the lookout for new books. They represent an excellent outlet for you to sell your book. At **Appendix D** you will find a list of independent bookstores that you can market to directly. If you choose to market to them directly send them a copy of your catalog. Do not send a copy of the book.

Black-owned bookstores are another source of independent bookstores. There are thousands of black-owned bookstores. These bookstores look for titles that are written by black authors or written about the black community. They represent another outlet for you sell your book. A list of black-owned independent bookstores is presented at **Appendix E**. If you choose to market to them directly send them a copy of your catalog. Do not send a copy of the book.

Airport Bookstores represents another category of independent bookstores. There are hundreds of airport bookstores throughout the United States and Canada. These bookstores, though small when compared to the likes of Borders and Barnes & Noble, offer an opportunity to sell thousands of books. You should consider this avenue to increase sales of your book.

When it comes to airport bookstores the peak selling times are summertime and the holiday season. Paperback books with a typical size of 6" x 9" are the type of book that airport bookstores like to carry. Shelf space is limited and paperback book tend to occupy less space. Business travelers and children are a good target audience to focus on.

The best way to market to airport bookstores is by approaching the distributors that serve them. In return for up to a 70% discount, distributors will promote your book to the retailers they serve. However, their payment terms may exceed 90 days. This is how long you will have to wait before you receive royalties from them. The benefit to this approach is that you only have to deal with a small number of entities, but the rewards for immediate national distribution can be significant.

When marketing to these distributors you should do the following:
- send a copy of your book
- include information about who is providing sales, marketing and distribution services on your behalf
- include a marketing plan (if requested)
- provide a copy of your catalog (see **Appendix H**)
- include in the catalog:
  - how many books are in a cartoon
  - how many units were published
  - list book reviews

Below is the list of distributors that you should promote your book to in order to get them sold in airport bookstores.

Airport bookstore distributors:

Bookazine and Anderson News
Attn: New Vendor Development Coordinator
Bookazine Co., Inc.
75 Hook Road
Bayonne, NJ 07002
http://www.bookzine.com
Complete submission guidelines for Bookazine may be found at:
http://www.bookazine.com/customer_service/instructions.shtml.

Bookazine requirements:

- book must have an ISBN and barcode with prince printed on it

- submit one copies of the book along with two sets of promotional materials (catalog)

- catalog information should include:
  - how many books are in a box and how many units are published
  - who is providing sales and marketing service on your behalf

National Distribution Network (NDN)
Attn: Gail Kump, VP, Business Development
4501 Forbes Blvd., Suite 200
Lanham, MD 20706
Ph: 301.459.3366
FAX: 301.429.5746
http://www.nbnbooks.com/ProspectivePublisher/
Email: gkump@nbnbooks.com

Requirements for NDN:

- Send copies of your title

- Completed prospective questionnaire

- Any recent advertising and reviews of your title

- Current catalog

The News Group West
Attn: New Vendor Review
3400 D Industry Drive East
Fife, Washington, 98424
253.922.8011
Fax: 253.896.5027
www.thenewsgroup.com
Email:
http://www2.thenewsgroup.com/US/Book_Vendor.htm

The News Group Requirements:

- The News Group do not consider publishers with 5 titles or less
- If you have more than 5 titles download forms at: **http://www.thenewsgroup.com/AreYouaVendor/Pages/BookVendorUS.aspx**

Paradies Shops
Attn: Alison Brown
5950 Fulton Industrial Boulevard SW
P O Box 43485

Atlanta GA 30336
404-344-7905
Fax: 404-349-7539
http://www.theparadiesshops.com
Email: **allison.brown@theparadiesshops.com**

Requirements for Paradies:

- Book must have an ISBN and barcode with prince printed on it

- Submit 1 copies of the book along with two sets of promotional materials (catalog)

- Catalog information should include:
    - how many books are in a box and how many units are published
    - Who is providing sales and marketing service on your behalf

CHAIN BOOKSTORES:

Barnes & Noble:
Visit the Barnes & Noble site at:
http://www.barnesandnoble.com/help/cds2.asp?PID=8148

One of two ways you can get your book into Barnes & Noble:

1. **Method #1 [Vendor of Record]:** You must become a Vendor of Record by completing a Publisher Information Form to establish a stocking relationship with the warehouse. Once this process is completed Barnes & Noble will place an order for two books.

2. **Method #2 [The Retail Store Placement]:** Submit a copy of the book (no manuscripts), along with marketing and promotion plans, trade reviews, and a note describing what makes the book unique, to:

        The Small Press Department
        Barnes & Noble, Inc.

122 Fifth Ave
New York, NY 10011

Books-A-Million:
Books-A-Million is the third largest book retailer in the nation with over 200 stores in 19 states and the District of Columbia. They also sell books on the Internet at
http://www.booksamillion.com.

Books-A-Million only accepts books that are carreid by one of the following distributors:

> American Wholesale Book Company
> Ingram Book Company
> Baker & Taylor

If your titles are carried by one of these distributors, you can send or email (marketing@booksamillion.com) the information to the attention of:

> Director of Merchandising
> Booksamillion.com
> P.O. Box 19728
> Birmingham, AL 35219

You can see the details about their program at:

> *http://www.booksamillion.com/publishers/books.h
> tml?id=4907416242851#consideratio*

Target:
Target has approximately 1,500 stores throughout the country. Getting your book into Target stores is a very difficult task. Target does not readily provide information on how to get your book into their stores. The best way to find out what it takes to get your book into Target is to obtain a Special Report by Mary Zable Fisher (of Zable Fisher Public Relations) for $49. The report is a result of investigative reporting and is available at:

http://www.zfpr.com/target.htm

Walmart:

Walmart stores have a complicated process, though not impossible. You must first become a Walmart Supplier. Procedures for getting your books into Walmart stores are outlined on their website at:

http://walmartstores.com/Suppliers/252.aspx

Steps to become a Walmart supplier will include these following.

1. Become familiar with Walmart and the way they operate. Visit their website and visit the store and learn as much as you can about the organization.
2. Obtain a Supplier Evaluation Report from Dunn & Bradstreet (D&B) at *http://smallbusiness.dnb.com.*
3. Complete the online submission packet.
4. Obtain a copy of the Product Liability Certificate of Insurance.
5. Obtain proof of barcode labeling or UPC.
6. If you are a minority/female owned business you will need to provide proof of certification.
7. Once the application is completed and submitted a Walmart buyer will contacted you. If they are interested they will ask you to provide a sample of your product.
8. If they decide to take you on as a vendor they will ask you to sign a contract.

Military Bookstores:

Army and Air Force Exchange Services (AAFES) sell products at 12,000 facilities worldwide, in catalogs, and online to active duty military, National Guard members, Reservists, and Retirees.

Their local distributors serving the area, in which the exchange is located, supply the majority of books and publications to exchanges. Contracts with distributors are on a guaranteed sales basis and require the contractor to provide in-store service and remove unsold and outdated publications.

If you wish to sell books and publications within the exchange, you should contact their distributors directly. Send a copy of your catalog. To see a list of distributors see **Appendix F** or visit this link:

http://www.shopmyexchange.com/DoingBusiness/retailsal es.htm

CHAPTER 13

BOOK PUBLISHING ASSOCIATIONS

Book Publishing Associations are excellent resources for the self-publisher. These organizations are located throughout the United States and provide the self-publisher with the opportunity to do the following:

- Network with other members in the organization from all aspects of the printing industry (such as writers, publishers, printers (POD), book buyers, book sellers, etc.)

- The opportunity to market books via their marketing programs which allow you to reach a significantly larger audience at very low cost.

- Provide educational opportunities through webinars and other training events that educate members on all aspects of publishing and marketing their book.

These organizations have regular meetings. Their membership comprises of members from all aspects of the publishing industry. They charge an annual membership fee.

Below is a listing of some of the most prominent book publishing associations that cater to self-publishers.

Independent Book Publishers Association (IBPA):
http://www.ibpa-online.org/

Membership: $119-$605

The IBPA offers great marketing opportunities for the self-publisher. Marketing programs include mailings to libraries, bookstores, reviewers, targeted mailings, etc. They will represent your book at book shows around the country for less than $100.

Colorado Independent Publishers Association (CIPA):
http://cipabooks.com

Membership Fees: $25-$185

CIPA has over 300 plus members. Meet monthly. They provide networking opportunities and encourage the free exchange of information. They assist members with the writing and marketing of their books.

Midwest Independent Publishers Association (MIPA):
http://www.mipa.org

Membership Fees: $25-$50

Serves the Midwest publishing community in a collaborative sharing of publishing, production, promotion, and marketing information.

Arizona Book Publishers Associations (ABPA):
http://azbookpub.com

Membership Fees: Not available

Arizona Book Publishing Association's mission is to advance and promote successful book publishing in Arizona through education, community involvement, cooperative effort, peer-recognition, industry advocacy. They also have over 150 publishers and associate members.

Association of Jewish Book Publishers (AJBP):
http://www.avotaynu.com/ajbp.html

Membership Fees: Not available

AJBP is a non-profit organization that promotes the sale and use of Jewish books through educational programs and activities such as exhibits, discussions, cooperative promotion and the interchange of information among members. The association provides a forum to discuss the mutual interests of publishers, authors and other individuals and institutions concerned with Jewish books. Jewish books span a wide range of topics, including religion, history, literature, cookbooks and children's books.

Bay Area Publishers Association (BAPA):
http://www.baipa.org

Membership Fees: $40

BAIPA is an educational institution dedicated to elevating the art of the self-publisher. They also provide educational programs, networking, marketing opportunities, and information on industry vendors and services and conduct monthly meetings.

Bookbuilders of Boston:
http://www.bbboston.org

Membership Fees: $350-$750

Bookbuilders of Boston is a nonprofit organization dedicated to bringing together people involved in book publishing and manufacturing throughout New England. They also provide information and resources for publishing professionals and conduct monthly networking meetings.

Bookbuilders West:
http://www.bookbuilders.org/wordpress/?page_id=26

Membership Fees: $50-$750

Bookbuilders West is an educational and professional organization that caters to members of the Western publishing community. They provide opportunities for participants to meet and share experiences at various educational and social activities. They also conduct an annual book show every January.

Members must be located in, or do business in, one of the 13 Western states: Alaska, Arizona, California, Colorado, Hawaii, Idaho, Montana, Nevada, New Mexico, Oregon, Utah, Washington, and Wyoming.

Chicago Book Clinic:
http://chicagobookclinic.org

Membership Fees: $25-$2,700

Chicago Book Clinic encourages excellence in publishing by providing a platform for educational, social and professional interaction of its members. Members are professionals in book and media publishing, printing, editorial, design, and all business aspects of the industry. They host a variety of educational programs, publications, and special events.

Evangelical Christian Publishers Association (ECPA):
http://www.ecpa.org

Membership Fees: $25-$15,000

ECPA is an international non-profit trade organization comprised of nearly 200 member companies worldwide that are involved in the publishing and distribution of Christian literature.

The Florida Publishers Association, Inc.:
http://www.flbookpub.org

Membership Fees: Not available

The Florida Publishers Association offers Florida's book publishers, self-publishers, authors and publishing vendors an opportunity for education and networking. They provide their members with support, and serve as a clearinghouse for up-to-date book publishing information. They accept members from all over the US and internationally.

Hawaii Publishers Association:
http://www.hawaiipublishersassociation.com

Membership Fees: Not available

Hawaii Publishers Association is a nonprofit media organization that promotes magazines, newspapers, books, and other aspects of the publishing industry in Hawaii. They also provide education and information to their members.

New England Publishes Association:
http://www.sitesys.com/draft/nepa/index.html

Membership Fees: Not available

The New England Publishers Association (NEPA) serves writers, authors and independent publishers. They conduct workshops, book displays and signings, cooperative programs with colleges & universities.

Small Publishers Association of North America (SPAN):
http://www.sacpublishers.com

Membership Fees: $0-$150

The mission of SPAN is to provide benefits that make our members more successful authors and publishers. SPAN members self publish books, and are also authors, writers, independent publishing companies, and nonprofit publishers.

Small Publishers, Artists and Writers Network (SPAWN):
http://www.spawn.org

Membership Fees: Not available

SPAWN provides information, resources and opportunities for everyone involved in or interested in publishing, whether you are an author, freelance writer, artist or you own a publishing company. They also encourage the exchange of ideas, information, and other mutual benefits.

Women's National Book Association (WNBA):
http://www.wnba-books.org

Membership Fee: Not available

The Women's National Book Association is a national organization of women and men who work with and value books. WNBA exists to promote reading and to support the role of women in the literary community. You can benefit from their networking and promotional opportunities.

Mid-Atlantic Book Publishers Association:
http://www.midatlanticbookpublishers.com/about

Membership Fee: $35-$350

A community of independent publishers located in the Mid-Atlantic area. They welcome all independent and self-publishers in Maryland, Delaware, Pennsylvania, Virginia, West Virginia, New Jersey, and Washington, DC.

Publishers Association of Los Angeles (PALA):
http://www.pa-la.org

Membership Fee: $75-$250

PALA membership is open to all publishers, vendors, and participants in the publishing industry in the greater Los Angeles area. Conducts educational and networking meetings.

Publishers & Writers of San Diego (PWSD):
http://www.publisherswriters.org

Membership Fee: Not available

The PWSD is composed of authors, self-publishers, editors, book packagers, designers, consultants, promotional professionals, students, and more. They also conducts educational and networking meetings.

Chicago Women in Business (CWIB):
http://www.cwip.org/resources/webdirectory.htm

Membership Fee: Not available

They meet monthly on the third Wednesday at the Willis (formerly Sears) Tower in downtown Chicago for networking and a career-related educational program. They also hold spring and fall receptions. Smaller groups also meet monthly in the city and the suburbs for informal networking get-togethers.

CHAPTER 14

E-BOOKS

The electronic form of your book -- otherwise known as e-book -- is one of the fastest growing segment of the publishing industry. Devices such as the Nook, IPAD, IPodKindle, Neo, Touch, Novell, Kobo, Cooler & Pocket Pro allow people to read an electronic version of your book. According to the Association of American Publishers, the publishing industry expects sales of e-books to account for $6 billion of the $20 billion book market by 2012.

There are three approaches you can take to convert and sell your book as an e-book. Which one you chose depends on how much effort you want to exert and how much royalties you are willing to part with.

The first option is to sign up with a **Digital Aggregator** and have them distribute your e-book to the major e-bookstores such as Apple iBookstore, Barnes & Noble, Borders, Amazon.com, Sony, etc. Through this option you will earn less royalties than if you went directly to each of the major e-book retailers. Digital Aggregators includes **Smashwords**, **Romeii Publishing** and **Borders Bookbrewer.com**. Royalty rates through these organizations can be as low as 41%. See below for more details on these Aggregators and their services.

The second option is to go to each of the major e-bookstore retailers and publish your book with them. Major e-bookstore retailers include **Amazon.com, Google, Barnes & Noble**, and **Apple iBookstore**. Royalty rates from the individual major e-bookstore retailers only go as low as 53%. See below for the details on each of the major e-bookstore retailers.

The third option is to utilize the ebook service from the "Printer" that you're using to get your book printed. Many of these on-demand service companies also provide ebook services that enables you to get your ebook printed and distributed to major ebook retailers.

AGGREGATORS:

SMASHWORDS (one-stop solution):

If you are looking for a one-stop solution SMASHBOOKS is one company that offers that type of solution. Through them you can get your e-book distributed to **Apple iBookstore, Barnes & Noble, Sony, Borders Kobo** and the **Diesel eBook Store**. Your book will also be available for sale on **Smashwords.com**.

You can access the program at:
http://www.**smashwords.com/signup?sony=yes**

Smashwords Royalty rates are as follows:
- 60% (from major eBook retailers)
- 85% (from listing on Smashbooks.com)
- 75.5% (from affiliate sales)

Smashwords also have an affiliate program that gives the affiliates 11% royalty. Affiliates are third party bloggers, web site operators, authors, publishers and Internet marketers that promote Smashwords books simply by hyperlinking to Smashwords pages.

You can create your book in MS Word and upload it to Smashwords as a word document.

ROMEII PUBLISHING (one-stop solution):

Romeii also offers a one-stop solution. They will convert and distributes your e-book to **Barnes & Noble, Sony.com, Kobo.com, and Borders Books**, **Apple iBookstore** and **Amazon Kindle**

You can access the program at:
http://ebooks.**romeii.com**

Cost: Charges a flat up-front fee of $200.00 and a $5.00 monthly maintenance fee.

Royalties: They do not take any percentage of the royalties. You will get full royalties as follows:

Barnes & Noble = 65% or 40%

Sony.com	= Not available
Kobo.co	= Not available
Borders Books	= 41%
Apple iBookstore	= 70%
Amazon	= 70%

File type: Romeii will accept your PDF, DOC, TXT or ZIP files
The book will be ready 72 hours after uploading it.

BOOKBREWER GET PUBLISHED SERVICE (one-stop solution):

Through **Bookbrewer.com program** you can get create your e-book and have it posted to multiple sites such as **Barnes & Noble, Amazon.com, iBookstore, Google Editions** and **Kobo.**

You can access the program at: http://bookbrewer**.com/home.**

Establishing the account is free and easy. Once you've created your book you can purchase one of their marketing program ($19.99 to $59.99) that will get you e-book listed on all of the above sites. With that program they will provide an ISBN for your e-book.

Royalties: Borders Bookbrewer.com will give you royalties depending on where the book was sold, as follows:

Amazon.com	=	49%
Barnes & Noble	=	49%
Apple iBookstore	=	53%

All e-books must be priced between $2.99 and $9.99. Borders Bookbrewer.com does not allow you to set a price lower than $2.99 or higher than $9.99. If you wish to sell you book at a higher price publish it at the individual sites of the major bookstores.

Bookbrewer.com requirements:

What do you need?
To upload your book you need a front cover and the contents of the book.

File size:
Image file must be no larger than 4MB and the resolution must be between 500 x 500 to 1000 x 1000 pixels.

File type:
To create your book you will **COPY** and **PASTE** it to the online location Chapter by Chapter. Hence, the contents of your document can be in **MS Word, EPUB** or any other content type.

The images for the front cover can be uploaded as a **JPEG,** or **JPG** file type.

File naming:
The only file you will upload is the image of the front cover. You can give that file any name you chose. There are no file naming conventions to abide by.

Formatting:
After the book (PDF file) is converted to an e-book (EPUB file) all page numbering will be removed and the rest of the document will appear just as it is in the PDF document. You can upload pictures into your document (using the camera icon) and resize the images by dragging the edges.

Once the text is uploaded you will be able to manipulate the font.

If you want to preview your book before publishing it you can do so with **Adobe Digital Editions**. You download and install a copy on your computer and use it to see what your book will look like once it is published. You can get a free copy of the software at: http://www.**adobe.com/products/digitaleditions/**.

You can also convert your Microsoft Word to an eBook reader by downloading and installing the plug-in for free from http://www.**microsoft.com/reader/developers/downloads/r mr.aspx**

MAJOR E-BOOKSTORE RETAILERS:

AMAZON.COM E-BOOK SERVICE:

To list your book as an e-book on amazon.com you have to open account (free) at https://dtp.**amazon.com**.

When you upload your book to the amazon.com site you will be able to view it in a Kindle display. This allows you to see how the book will appear to readers who buy it. If you are not satisfied with the way it looks you can edit it and upload it again before making it available for sale.

Amazon.com has a feature called "look inside" which allow viewers to browse approximately 20% of the book for free before buying it.

Royalties: Amazon.com have a 35% or 70% royalty option. To get the 70% royalty books must be priced at $9.95 or less. Books sold over $9.95 utilize the 35% royalty option.

You set the retail price for your book.

Amazon.com requirements:

What do you need?
To upload your book you need a front cover, and the contents of the book.

File size:
There is no limit on the size of the file, but it should be at least 600 x 800 pixels. The file should be zipped before uploading. The front cover can be a separate file, but the contents of the book, including any images that part of the content should be zipped as one file. If you don't have the software to zip your file you can find one at http://www.**winzip.com**. It only cost $29.95. Image and content must be zipped in the same folder, without any sub-folders.

File type:
The content files can be submitted as an HTML file. The images for the front and back cover can be uploaded as a GIF, JPEG, PNG or BMP file type.

Amazon.com e-books are displayed in black & white for the Kindle and color for Kindle apps on I-phone or PC.

File naming:
You can give the file any name you desire.
Dimensions:
No limitations on dimensions.

Formatting:
After the book is converted to an e-book all page numbering will be removed. The first line of every paragraph will be automatically indented once uploaded and converted. Text in bold or italics will be retained after conversion. When you format the file in HTML you have to remove all blank pages, page numbers and Index.

Do not set margins (top, bottom, left or right). You can convert your Microsoft word document to an HTML document simply by saving it as an HTML document (click on **FILE → SAVE AS →** in the window that opens chose the HTML option from the **SAVE AS TYPE** field).

If you use "**Normal(Web)**" font your file will look exactly the same as it would when converted to the Amazon (AZW) file standard or an EPUB file standard.

GOOGLE EDITIONS:

The Google e-book program works in conjunction with the Google Partner program. The Google Partner program is free. To convert your book to an e-book all you have to do is upload your book to Google Partner then select the option to make your book an e-book. To convert the book to an e-book, follow these steps:

Under the "**Google Editions** tab**→** click on **Show e-books →** then click on the **pencil icon** next to the book you want to convert to an e-book **→** then click in the **STATUS** check box **to enable Google Editions Sales for the Title**.

Your e-book will be displayed at the Google e-bookstore (http://books**.google.com/ebook**s). Their retail partners will also be able to sell them on their own sites. As a result your book will get enormous exposure.

You do not have to establish an e-commerce site to sell your e-books on Google. They will handle all of that for you. However, in order to sell your book as a hard copy through your Google Partner account you will be asked to provide a URL (web address) that visitors can click on to order your book.

Also, on your Partner account you will be able to tell Google to display a certain percent of your book for visitors to browse freely in order to learn what the book is about. For example, you can tell it to only display 20% of the book.

Royalties: Google will pay you 52% of the list price in royalties. Google will share the revenue from any sales with you according to the list price that you provide. Google and its authorized resellers have the discretion to set prices as they see fit.

You can sign up for a Google Partner account at:
http://www.**google.com/googlebooks/tour/**.

The control panel for your Partner account allows you to view reports that show details on how many people view or buy your book for any given month.

Google requirements:

What do you need?
To upload your book you need a front cover, back cover and the contents of the book.

File size:
Cannot be less than six (6) pages. To upload online the file must be less than 20MB. Files larger than 20MB must be sent in on CD/DVD.

File type:
The content files can be submitted as PDF or EPUB. The images for the front and back cover can be uploaded as a PDF, JPG, JPEG or TIF file type.

File naming:
File names must include the ISBN (ISBN_content.pdf). Dashes should not be included in the file name. For example:
>- 123456789_content.pdf = for the content
>- 123456789_frontcover.pfd = for the front cover
>- 123456789_backcover.pdf = for the back cover

Dimensions:
Cannot be more than 11.7" in one dimension. No limit in the other direction. Cannot be smaller than 1.9" x 2.75".

Formatting: after the book (PDF file) is converted to an e-book (EPUB file) all page numbering will be removed and the rest of the document will appear just as it is in the PDF document.

Payments:
To get paid your e-book royalties you have to link your Google account with a bank account. You do this under the **My Account** tab.

Reports:
Google Editions will provide a monthly report on your e-book in your Partner account.

BARNES & NOBLE:

Sign up for an account at:
http://pubit.**barnesandnoble.com/pubit_app/bn?t=pi_reg_home**

Signing up for the account is free and very easy. However, during the sing up process you will be asked to provide your banking information (routing & account number). This is how you will get paid from the sales of your book. You will also be required to provide credit card information. This is to be used in those instances where you are over-paid and Barnes & Noble need to re-coop their money.

You do not have to establish an e-commerce site to sell your e-books on Barnes & Noble. They will handle all of that for you.

Barnes & Noble offer the following features with their service:
- Browse up to one hour
- A buyer can lend the book to a friend for up to 14 days. It will not be available to him/her while it is on loan.
- Try before they buy: Download up to 5% of the book for free.

Once published, the book will be available within 24-72 hours.

Royalties: Barnes & Noble will pay you 65% of the list price in royalties if the listed price is between $2.99 and $9.99, and 40% of list price if the book is listed at less than $2.98 and over $10.00. You can set the list price or let Barnes & Noble set the list price. Barnes & Noble reserve the right to change the list price. If you list your e-book on other sites you must ensure that the Barnes & Noble list price is not greater than what you list it for on other sites.

Barnes & Noble requirements:

What do you need?
To upload your book you need a front cover and the contents of the book.

File size:
To upload online the file must be less than 20MB.

File type:
The content files can be submitted as an EPUB file. A free tool is available at "Pubit" to convert your file to an EPUB format. You can also find EPUB conversion tools at:

Calibre – convert PDF to EPUB (Cost: Free)
http://calibre-**ebook.com**

AVS Document Converter – Convert to any file type (Cost: Free)
http://www.avs4you.com/AVS-Document-Converter.aspx

2EPUB – Convert PDF, TXT or Word to EPUB (Cost: $Free)
http://www.2epub.com

The images for the front and back cover can be uploaded as a JPEG or JPG file type. It must be between 5KB and 2MB in size. It must be between 750 and 2000 pixels.

File naming: No restrictions on naming your files.

Formatting: Utilize the free tool available on Pubit to convert your file to an EPUB file then edit it before uploading. Formatting includes support for: bold, italics, underline, strikethrough, etc., Internal & External Links, Indentation, Bulleted lists Numbered lists and Tables, etc. If you use "**Normal(Web)**" font your file will look exactly the same as it would when converted to an EPUB file. You can edit the book after it is published, however, you cannot edit the ISBN.

Payments:
To get paid you have to link your Pubit account with a bank account. You do this during the account setup process. You can edit this information later from the Pubit control panel after you login.

Reports:
You can view reports on your titles at the Pubit site under the "MY SALES" tab.

APPLE IBOOKSTORE:

1. First you need An Intel-based Mac running OS X 10.5 or later

2. You also need QUICKTIME 7.0.3 or later installed on your computer.

3. **Open an iTunes Account:** Download and Install iTunes

> For Windows XP:
>
> http://www.**techspot.com/downloads/70-apple-itunes-for-windows.html**

> For MAC:
>
> http://www.**apple.com/itunes/download/**

4. **Open iTunes** then click on **STORE** then select **CREATE ACCOUNT**. Follow the prompts and provide the requested information to complete the process. You will be asked to provide credit card information.

5. **Open a Publishing Account:** Visit this link and follow the instructions on the screen. You will need your iTunes account information to complete this part of the process. Use this link to open a publishing account:

https://itunesconnect.**apple.com/WebObjects/iTunesConnect.woa/wa/apply**

Additionally you will require the following:

- must have Tax ID (if you don't have one you can request one from the IRS at:

http://www.**irs.gov/businesses/small/article/0,,id=97860,00.html**

- must have ISBN.

Follow the instructions on the website to begin publishing.

Royalties:
Apple will give publishers/authors 70% of list price as royalties.

iBookstore requirements:

What do you need?
To upload your book you need a front cover and the contents of the book.

File size:
Limit file size to 20MB or less.

File type:
The content files can be submitted as an .EPUB file. You can also find EPUB conversion tools at:

Calibre – convert PDF to EPUB (Cost: Free)
http://calibre-**ebook.com**

AVS Document Converter – Convert to any file type (Cost: Free)
http://www.**avs4you.com/AVS-Document-Converter.aspx**

2EPUB – Convert PDF, TXT or Word toEPUB (Cost: $Free)
http://www.**2epub.com**

The images for the front and back cover can be uploaded as a JPEG or JPG file type. It must be between 5KB and 2MB in size. It must be between 750 and 2000 pixels.

File naming:
No restrictions on naming your files.

Formatting: Convert your file to an EPUB file then edit it before uploading. Formatting includes support for: bold, italics, underline, strikethrough, etc., Internal & External Links, Indentation, Bulleted lists Numbered lists and Tables, etc.

If you use "**Normal(Web)**" font your file will look exactly the same as it would when converted to an EPUB file. You cannot edit the book after it is published.

Payments:
To get paid you have to link your account to a bank account. You do this during the account setup process. You can edit this information later from the control panel after you login.

SONY:
http://ebookstore.**sony.com/publishers/**

To self-publish your e-book to the Sony store you have to use one of their Digital Aggregator:

Smashwords
http://www.smashwords.com/signup?sony=yes

Author Solutions
http://www.authorsolutions.com/Sony.aspx

PRINT ON DEMAND COMPANIES:

CREATESPACE:
Createspace teamed up with amazon.com to provide ebook service. If you use Createspace as your print-on-demand company the only thing you have to do after uploading your book in .PDF format to get it converted to an ebook and sold on amazon.com is to check a couple of boxes then logon to amazon.com and check a few boxes. That's all. The program is called Kindle Direct Publishing (KDP). You can access it at https://kdp-amazon.com/self-publish. You must setup an account on amazon-kindle. Don't publish your ebook elsewhere before using KDP. You have to provide an ISBN for the ebook. It cost nothing. Your ebook will be available in many countries.

LULU:
In addition to their print-on-demand service Lulu also offers an ebook service. However, their service requires you to first use their tool to convert the book to an ebook format. After publishing with Lulu your ebook can appear on Barnes & Noble and iBookstore. The service is free. Visit: http://www.lulu.com/publish/ebooks/free.

LIGHTNINGSOURCE:
LightningSource also offers an ebook service in addition to their pring-on-demand service. However, it does require you to use your own efile conversion tool to create and upload the ePUB file. You can find more information here: http://www.lulu.com/publish/ebooks/free.

CHAPTER 15

PROMOTE THE BOOK - RADIO SHOWS & BLOGS

You should have as a key objective, bringing attention to your book. One of the least expensive ways to do this is to appear on talk shows and talk about your book to a wide audience. There are many radio talk shows that are dedicated to giving you the opportunity to do just that for free.

Below is a listing of radio talk shows that you can use to promote your book. These shows are broadcasted over the Internet or the airwaves or both. You should tune in and listen before making your appearance.

The KC Girlfriends Book Club Radio Show (KCGBC):
http://www.blogtalkradio.com/kcgirlfriendsbookclub

This Show is a radio program that supports new or underexposed African American (AA) authors with good books! KCGBC also holds panel discussions with sister book clubs from around the country and literary resources. The show airs Mondays and Wednesdays at 8:00 p.m. EST over the Internet.

The Black Authors Network (BAN):
http://www.blogtalkradio.com/black-author-network

The Black Authors Network (BAN) is dedicated to providing information to help black business owners and authors gain access to the global consumer and to helping promote the growth of black businesses and literature. It airs Mondays and Wednesdays at 8:00 p.m. EST over the Internet. Visit the website to learn more about becoming a guest and listening to the show.

From Cover to Cover Literary Talk Show:
http://www.fromcovertocovershow.com

This show explores aspects of the literary industry and provides a venue for authors to expand their audience and readership through the powerful medium of FM Radio and the Internet. The show's format is a combination of informative literary news stories, topic-driven segments, and live author interviews. Visit the website to learn about upcoming shows and to listen to previously aired shows. To become a guest on the show, send an electronic press kit to Executive Producer, **Ron Reynolds** (*covertocovershow@aol.com*) and allow up to 48 hours to acknowledge receipt.

African Americans on the Move (AAMBC) Radio :
http://www.blogtalkradio.com/aambc

This is a show-stopper for all authors and is syndicated on a national online radio show, reaching thousands of listeners. Every second and last Friday of the month they host Author Exposure Interviews. They also have special author interviews to be scheduled when requested. Authors and poets are invited to call in on monthly Open Mic Shows to share book synopses or poems. The show airs every Friday at 7:30 p.m. EST. Visit the website to learn about upcoming shows and to listen to previously aired shows and learn more about becoming a guest on the show.

Your15Minutes Radio:
http://www.blogtalkradio.com/your15minutes

Your 15 Minutes Radio Show is a show that gives individuals 15 minutes to promote their products and services. Interested in being on the show? Email guest at **www.your15minutesradio.com**. The show airs live every Tuesday at 6 p.m. CST/7 p.m. EST. If you want to be a guest visit them at *Guest@Your15MinutesRadio.com*. Visit the website to learn about upcoming shows, listen to previously aired shows and learn more about to become a guest on the show.

Literary Pizzazz:
http://www.blogtalkradio.com/literarypizzazz

This show features authors, publishers, young writers and spoken word artists. Literary Pizzazz gives voice to the unsung authors or rising entrepreneurs. If interested in becoming a guest send a personal message (to *Pam Osbey at* **mocha.sistah@gmail.com**) with "**Show Bookings**" in the subject line. You must send a copy book to be reviewed at least 1-2 weeks before your interview. Visit the website to learn about upcoming shows, listen to previously aired shows and learn more about becoming a guest on the show.

BLOGS

Blogs are a great way to get tips on selling your book. You should subscribe to several blogs and tune in regularly to hear what everyone else is saying. Below are some recommended book blogs.

The Savvy Book Mrketer:
http://bookmarketingmaven.typepad.com

Independent Book Marketing Group:
http://www.independentbookmarketinggroup.com

BookMarketingBuzzBlog:
http://bookmarketingbuzzblog.blogspot.com

Market Your Book:
http://marketyourbookblog.com/blog/

Book Marketing@tweetYourBook:
https://twitter.com/TweetYourBook

Brian Jud@bookmarketing:
https://twitter.com/bookmarketing

APPENDIX A

ISBN/BARCODE DISPLAY

Sample display of the ISBN on the copyright page:

Sample display of the Barcode on the back book cover:

The best resource for the Entrepreneur. Now millions who contemplate starting new small businesses every year have a useful resource that they can turn to for information. This resource bring all the information you need to start and run a small business to your finger tips.

Recommended Reasings:

12 Factors of Business Success: by Kevin Hogan & David Lakhani & Mollie Marti, Published by Wiley, John & Sons, Inc. [$24.95]

Business Law: by Robert W. Emerson, J.D., Published by Barron's [$25.99]

The Small Business Valuation Book: by Lawrence W. Tuller, Published by Adams Mdia [$16.50]

From Concept to Consumer: by Phil Baker Published by FT Press [$24.99]

Strategic Thinking: by Andy Bruce & Ken Langdon, Published DK Publishing, Inc. [$7.00]

The E-Myth Revisited: Why most Small Businesses Don't Work and wht to do About it, by Michael E. Gerber, Published by Harper Collins [$16.95]

A Girl's Guide to Building A Million-Dollar Business by Susan Wilson Solovic, Published by AMACOM [$21.95]

Printed in the U.S.A.
www.createspace.com
www.sbzbooks.com
www.sbz1.com
www.amazon.com

$19.95
ISBN 978-0-9829036-5-0
51995>

9 780982 903650

APPENDIX B

MAJOR NEWSPAPERS REVIEW PROGRAM

The Arizona Republic
http://www.azcentral.com/help/articles/contact.html

Anchorage Daily News
http://www.adn.com

Atlanta Journal-Constitution
http://projects.ajc.com/search/?term=book+editor

Austin American Statesman
http://www.statesman.com

Baltimore Sun
http://www. baltimoresun.com

The Baton Rouge Advocate
http://www.2theadvocate.com

Boston Globe
http://www.boston.com

Boston Herald
http://www.bostonherald.com

Buffalo News
http://www.buffalonews.com

Charlotte Observer
www.charlotteobserver.com/books

Chicago Sun-Times
http://www.suntimes.com

Chicago Tribune
http://www.chicagotribune.com

Publishers Weekly
http://www.publishersweekly.com

Christian Science Monitor
http://www.csmonitor.com

Cincinnati Enquirer
http://news.enquirer.com

Cleveland Plain Dealer
http://www.cleveland.com

Contra Costa Times
http://www.contracosta times.com

The Denver Post
http://www. denverpost.com

Detroit Free Press
http://www.freep.com

South Florida Sun-Sentinel
http://www.sun-sentinel.com/features/booksmags

Fort Worth Star-Telegram
http://www.star-telegram.com

Hartford Courant
http://www.courant.com

The Honolulu Advertiser
http://www.honoluluadvertiser.com

Houston Chronicle
http://www.chron.com

Indianapolis Star
http://www.indystar.com

Kansas City Star
http://www.kcstar.com

Louisville Courier-Journal
http://www.courier-journal.com

Miami Herald
http://www.herald.com

Milwaukee Journal Sentinel
http://www.jsonline.com

Minneapolis Star Tribune
http://www.startribune.com

Nashville Tennessean
http://www.tennessean.com

New Orleans Times-Picayune
http://www.timespicayune.com

New York Post
http://www.nypost.com/news/opinion/books

Newark Star-Ledger
http://www.starledger.com

The Oregonian
http://www.oregonlive.com

Orlando Sentinel
http://www.orlandosentinel.com

Philadelphia Inquirer
http://www.philly.com

Pittsburgh Post-Gazette
http://www.post-gazette.com

Pittsburgh Tribune-Review
http://www.pittsburghlive.com

Sacramento Bee
http://www.sacbee.com

Saint Louis Post-Dispatch
http://www.stltoday.com

Saint Petersburg Times
http://www.sptimes.com

Salt Lake Tribune
http://www.sltrib.com

San Antonio Express-News
http://www.express-news.net

San Diego Union-Tribune
http://www.uniontrib.com

San Francisco Chronicle
http://www.sfgate.com

San Jose Mercury News
http://www.mercurynews.com/books

Santa Fe New Mexican
http://www.santafenewmexican.com

Seattle Times
http://www.seattletimes.com

Tampa Tribune
http://www.tampatrib.com

Washington Post Book World
http://www.washingtonpost.com

Washington Times
http://www.washingtontimes.com

USA Today
http://www.usatoday.com

Wall Street Journal
http://www.wsj.com

New York Times Book Review
http://www.nytimes.com/books

APPENDIX C

STATES LIBRARY CONTACTS

(You can buy this mailing list at:

http://sbzshop.corecommerce.com/MAILING-LIST/)

Alabama Public Library Service Attn: State Librarian 6030 Monticello Drive Montgomery, AL 36130	Hawaii State Library Attn: State Librarian 478 South King Street Honolulu, HI 96813-2994
Alaska State Library and Historical Collections Attn: State Librarian PO Box 110571 Juneau, AK 99811-0571	Idaho Commission of Libraries Attn: State Librarian 325 W State St. Boise, ID 83702
Arizona State Library Attn: State Librarian History and Archives Division 1901 W. Madison Phoenix, AZ 85009	Illinois State Library Attn: State Librarian Gwendolyn Brooks Building 300 South 2nd Street Springfield, IL 62701-1796
Arkansas State Library Attn: State Librarian One Capitol Mall Little Rock, AR 72201	Indiana State Library Attn: State Librarian 315 W. Ohio St. Indianapolis, IN 46202
California State Library Attn: State Librarian P.O. Box 942837 Sacramento, CA 94237-0001	Iowa State Library Attn: State Librarian Miller Building 1112 E. Grand Ave. Des Moines, IA 50319
Colorado State Library Attn: State Librarian 201 East Colfax Ave. Room 309 Denver, CO 80203	State Library of Kansas Attn: State Librarian Capitol Building, Room 343-N 300 SW 10th Avenue Topeka, KS 66612-1593
Connecticut State Library Connecticut State Library 231 Capitol Avenue Hartford, CT 06106	Kentucky State Library Attn: State Librarian P.O. Box 537 Frankfort, KY 40602-0537
District of Columbia Public Library Attn: State Librarian 901 G St. N.W. Washington, DC 20001	Louisiana State Library Attn: State Librarian P.O. Box 131 Baton Rouge, LA 70821
Florida State Library R.A. Gray Building Attn: State Librarian 500 South Bronough Street Tallahassee, FL 32399-0250	Maine State Library Attn: State Librarian 64 State House Station Augusta, ME 04333-0064
Georgia Public Library	Maryland State Library

Attn: State Librarian 1800 Century Place Suite 150 Atlanta, GA 30345-4304	Attn: State Librarian Sailor Operations Center 400 Cathedral Street Baltimore, MD 21201
Massachusetts Board of Library Commissioners Attn: State Librarian 98 North Washington St., Suite 401 Boston, MA 02114	New Mexico State Library Attn: State Librarian 1209 Camino Carlos Rey Santa Fe, NM 87507-5166
Michigan State Library Attn: State Librarian 702 West Kalamazoo Street Lansing, MI 48915-1609	New York State Library Attn: State Librarian 310 Madison Avenue Empire State Plaza Albany, NY 12230
Minnesota State Library Attn: State Librarian [Susan Miller] 1500 Highway 36 West Roseville, MN 55113	North Carolina State Library Attn: State Librarian 109 East Jones Street Raleigh, NC 27601-1023
Mississippi Library Commission Attn: State Librarian 3881 Eastwood Drive Jackson, MS 39211-6439	North Dakota State Library Attn: State Librarian 604 E. Boulevard Ave - Dept 250 Bismarck, ND 58505-0800
Missouri State Library Attn: State Librarian 600 W. Main St. P.O. Box 387 Jefferson City, MO 65101	Ohio State Library Attn: State Librarian 274 East 1st Avenue, Suite 100 Columbus, OH 43201-3692
Montana State Library Attn: Darlene Staffeldt, State Librarian P.O. Box 201800 1515 East 6th Avenue Helena MT 59620-1800	Oklahoma Department of Libraries 200 N.E. 18th St. Oklahoma City, OK 73105
Nebraska Library Commission Attn: State Librarian The Atrium 1200 N Street, Suite 120 Lincoln, NE 68508-2023	Oregon State Library Attn: State Librarian 250 Winter St. NE Salem, OR 97301-3950
Nevada State Library and Archives Attn: State Librarian 100 North Stewart Street Carson City, NV 89701-4285	Pennsylvania Department of Education Attn: State Librarian 333 Market Street Harrisburg, PA 17126-0333
New Hampshire State Library Attn: State Librarian 20 Park Street Concord, NH 03301	Office of Library & Information Svcs RI Department of Administration Attn: State Librarian One Capitol Hill, 2nd Floor Providence, RI 02908-5803
New Jersey State Library Attn: State Librarian P.O. Box 520 Trenton, NJ 08625-0520	South Carolina State Library Attn: State Librarian P.O. Box 11469 Columbia, SC 29211

South Dakota State Library Attn: State Librarian Mercedes MacKay Building 800 Governors Drive Pierre, SD 57501-2294	Vermont State Librarian Attn: Martha Reid, State Librarian Department of Libraries 109 State St. Montpelier, VT 05609-0601
Tennessee State Library and Archives Attn: State Librarian 403 7th Avenue North Nashville, TN 37243	Washington State Library Attn: State Librarian PO BOX 42460 Olympia, WA 98504-2460
Texas State Library & Archives Commission Attn: State Librarian P.O. Box 12927 Austin, TX 78711	West Virginia State Library Commission Attn: State Librarian 1900 Kanawha Blvd. E., Bldg. 9, Culture Center Charleston, WV 25305
The Library of Virginia Attn: State Librarian 800 East Broad Street Richmond, VA 23219	Wisconsin State Library Attn: State Librarian 125 S. Webster Street, P.O. Box 7841 Madison, WI 53707-7841
Utah State Library Division Attn: State Librarian 250 North, 1950 West, Suite A Salt Lake City, UT 84116-7901	Wyoming State Library Attn: State Librarian 2800 Central Avenue Cheyenne, WY 82002

Starting 15 January 2012 you can purchase library mailing lists for States for $9.99 by visiting the SBZ Shop at *http://www.shopsbz.com* and look under the "**MAILING LIST**" category.

Starting 15 January 2012 you can also purchase a marketing matrix for $9.99 which list all of the marketing tasks and allow you to choose your marketing task, track cost, and track the status. Visit the SBZ Shop at *http://www.shopsbz.com* and look under the "**BOOK MARKETING**" category.

APPENDIX D

INDEPENDENT BOOKSTORES LISTING

(You can buy this mailing list at:

http://sbzshop.corecommerce.com/MAILING-LIST/)

Abella Books PO Box 900352 Sandy, UT 84090-0352	http://www.abellabooks.com
Ambassador Books and Media 160 Finn Court Farmingdale, NY 11735, USA	http://www.absbook.com
Booksamillion.com Sales and Support P.O. Box 19728 Birmingham, AL 35211	http://www.booksamillioninc.com
Brown Book Shop 1517 San Jacinto Houston, TX 77002	http://www.brownbookshop.com/Contactus.html
Moe's Books 2476 Telegraph Avenue Berkeley CA 94704	http://moesbooks.com
Black Oak Books Holdings Corp. 1491 Shattuck Avenue Berkeley, CA, U.S.A. 94709	http://www.blackoakbooks.com
Mostly Books 6208 E. Speedway Blvd. Tucson, AZ 85712	http://www.mostlybooks.biz
Hearthside Books & Toys Nugget Mall 8745 Glacier Hwy Juneau, AK 99801	hearthside@hearthsidebooks.com
Parnassus Books 5 Creek Street Upstairs Ketchikan, AK 99901	http://www.ketchikanbooks.com
Alabama Booksmith 2626 19th Place, South Birmingham, AL 35209	http://www.alabamabooksmith.com/NASApp/store/IndexJsp
Eclipse Coffee & Books 1032 Main Street Montevallo, AL 35115	http://www.eclipsecoffee.com/contact.htm

The Well Red Coyote 3190 West Highway 89A, #400 Sedona, AZ 86336	http://wellredcoyote.com/contact.htm l
Rainy Faye's Bookstore 1402 Broad Street SUITE 130 Bridgeport, CT. 06604	http://www.anthology.com/rainyfaye/ wc.dll?main~bd
Barrett Bookstore Noroton Heights Shopping Center 314 Heights Road Darien, CT 06820	http://www.barrettbookstore.com/NA SApp/store/IndexJsp
Enterprise Books 326 Court Square DeWitt, AR 72042	http://www.enterprisebooksdewitt.co m
Books, Inc. 1501 Vermont Street, San Francisco, CA 94107; 415-643- 3400.	http://www.booksinc.net/about-us
Bookworks Aptos 36 Rancho Del Mar Center Aptos, CA 95003	http://www.bookworksaptos.com/NA SApp/store/IndexJsp
Pegasus Books Downtown 2349 Shattuck Avenue Berkeley, CA	http://www.pegasusbookstore.com
The Bookery Nook 4280 Tennyson Street Denver, CO 80212	http://www.thebookerynook.com/Con tact/
Explore Booksellers & Bistro 221 East Main Street Aspen, CO 81611	http://explorebooksellers.com
The Bookies 4315 E Mississippi Ave Denver, CO 80246	http://www.netnewsdesk.com/theboo kies/
Bethany Beach Books Box 904 99 Garfield Parkway Bethany Beach, DE 19930	http://www.bethanybeachbooks.com
Booksandcoffee ± Ruddertowne 124 Dickinson Street Dewey Beach, DE 10071	http://www.deweybooksandcoffee.co m

Presse Bookstore 1614 Wisconsin Avenue, NW Washington, DC 20007	http://www.pressebooks.com
Reiter's Books 1990 K St., NW (enter on 20th Street) Washington, D.C. 20006	http://www.reiters.com
Books & Books 265 Aragon Avenue Coral Gables, FL 33134	http://www.booksandbooks.com/NASApp/store/IndexJsp
Downtown Book Center, Inc. 247 SE 1st Street Miami, FL 33131	http://yp.bellsouth.com/sites/downtownbooks/
Eagle Eye Book Shop 2076 N. Decatur Road Decatur, GA 30033	http://www.eagleeyebooks.com/NASApp/store/IndexJsp
BOOKS NEVER-ENDING 2547 Cloud Springs Road Rossville, GA 30741	http://www.booksneverending.com/index.html?pageid=3
Iconoclast Books 671 sun valley road P.O. Box 806 Ketchum, ID 83340	http://www.iconoclastbooks.com
Rediscovered Bookshop 7079 Overland Road Boise, ID 83709	http://www.rdbooks.org
Barbara's Bookstore 1218 S. Halsted Street Chicago, IL 60607	http://www.barbarasbookstore.com
Lake Forest Bookstore 680 N. Western Ave. Lake Forest, IL 60045	http://www.lakeforestbookstore.com
The Book Stall at Chestnut Court 811 Elm Street Winnetka, IL 60093	http://www.thebookstall.com
Viewpoint Books 548 Washington Street Columbus, IN 47201	http://www.viewpointbooks.com
Three Sisters Books & Gifts, LLC 7 Public Square Shelbyville, IN 46176	http://www.threesistersbooks.com

Watermark Book & Café 4701 East Douglas Wichita, KS 67218	http://www.watermarkbooks.com
Town Crier 716 Commercial Emporia, KS 66801	http://www.towncrierbookstore.com
The Blue Marble 1356 South Fort Thomas Avenue Fort Thomas, KY 41075	http://site.booksite.com/5792/
Carmichael's Bookstore 1295 Bardstown Road Louisville, KY 40204	http://www.carmichaelsbookstore.com
Octavia Books 513 Octavia St New Orleans, LA 70115-2055	http://www.octaviabooks.com/index.php
Garden District Book Shop 2727 Prytania Street New Orleans, LA 70130	http://www.gardendistrictbookshop.com/NASApp/store/IndexJsp
Blue Hill Books 26 Pleasant Street Blue Hill, ME 04614	http://www.bluehillbooks.com
Longfellow Books One Monument Way Portland, ME 04101	http://www.longfellowbooks.com
Red Emma's Bookstore Coffee House 800 St. Paul St. Baltimore, MD 21202	http://www.redemmas.org
Book Nook Bookstore 5606 Baltimore Avenue Hyattsville, MD 20781	http://www.booknookbookstore.com
Amherst Books 8 Main Street Amherst, MA 01002 · ·	http://www.amherstbooks.com/AboutUs.shtml
Trident Booksellers &Cafe 338 Newbury Street Boston, MA 02115	http://www.tridentbookscafe.com

Marwil Bookstore 4870 Cass Avenue Detroit, MI 48201	http://marwilbookstore.liveonatt.com
Schuler Books and Music, Inc. 2660 28th Street SE Grand Rapids, MI 49512	http://www.schulerbooks.com
Central Avenue Bookstore 229 Central Avenue Faribault, MN 55021	http://www.centralavenuebooks.com
Northern Lights Books and Gifts 307 Canal Park Dr. Duluth, MN 55802	http://www.norlights.com
Lemuria Books 4506 Office Park Drive Jackson, MS 39206	http://www.lemuriabooks.com/index. php?show=about
Square Books 111 Courthouse Square Oxford, MS 38655	http://www.squarebooks.com
Reading Reptile 328 W. 63rd Street Kansas City, MO 64113	http://www.readingreptile.com/main/ about.htm
Coffee Break Book Store 322 Buss Lane Pineville, MO 64856	http://www.coffeebreakbookstore.com
Barjon's Books, Music & Gifts 223 North 29th Street Billings, MT 59101	http://www.barjonsbooks.com
Books & Books 206 W. Park St. Butte, MT 59701	http://www.butteamerica.com/books. htm
Seward Chapters 548 Seward Street Seward, NE 68434	www.sewardchapters.com
Lee Booksellers 5500 S. 56th St. Lincoln, NE 68516	http://www.leebooksellers.com
Sundance Bookstore and Music 1155 W. Fourth St. Suite 106 Reno, NV 89503	http://www.sundancebookstore.com

Gibson's Bookstore 27 South Main Street Concord, NH 03301	http://www.gibsonsbookstore.com
Morgan Hill Bookstore P.O. Box 2455 253 Main Street New London, NH 03257	http://www.morganhillbookstore.com
Montclair Book Center 221 Glenridge Ave. Montclair, NJ 07042	http://www.montclairbookcenter.com
The Town Book Store 270 E. Broad St. Westfield, NJ 07090	http://www.townbookstore.com
Moby Dickens Bookshop 124A Bent Street #6 Dunn House Taos, NM 87571	www.mobydickens.com
Tome on The Range 158 Bridge Street (Old Town) Las Vegas, NM 87701	http://www.tomeontherange.com
Brownstone Books 409 Lewis Avenue Brooklyn, NY 11233	http://www.brownstonebooks.com
The BookMark Shoppe 8415 3rd Avenue Brooklyn, NY 11209	http://www.bookmarkshoppe.com/NASApp/store/IndexJsp
Park Road Books 4139 Park Road Park Road Shopping Center Charlotte, NC 28209	http://www.parkroadbooks.com/NASApp/store/IndexJsp
Joseph-Beth Booksellers - Charlotte 4345 Barclay Downs Drive Charlotte, NC 28209	http://www.josephbeth.com
Main Street Books 106 South Main Street Minot, ND 58701	http://mainstbooks.booksense.com
Books 'N' More 28 W. Main Street Wilmington, OH 45177	http://bmore.shopping.officelive.com/default.aspx

Beehive Books 25 N. Sandusky St. Delaware, OH 43015	http://www.beehiveat25.com
Visible Voice Books 1023 Kenilworth Cleveland, OH 44113	http://www.visiblevoicebooks.com
Full Circle Bookstore 1900 NW Expressway Oklahoma City, OK 73118	http://www.fullcirclebooks.com
Steve's Sundry, Books & Magazines 2612 S. Harvard Tulsa, OK 74114	http://www.stevessundrybooksmags.com
Annie Bloom's Books 7835 SW Capital Highway Portland, OR 97219	http://www.annieblooms.com
St. Johns Bookseller 8622 N. Lombard St. Portland, OR 97203	http://stjohnsbooks.com
The Blue Marble Bookstore 551 Carpenter Lane Philadelphia, PA 19119	http://www.bigbluemarblebooks.com
Joseph Fox Bookshop 1724 Sansom Street Philadelphia, PA 19103	http://www.foxbookshop.com
Books On The Square 471 Angell Street Providence, RI 02906	http://www.booksq.com
Barrington Books 184 County Road Barrington, RI 02806	http://www.barringtonbooks.com
The Open Book 110 South Pleasantburg Drive Greenville, SC 29607	http://www.theopenbookonline.com
Booksmith Dogwood Plaza Seneca, SC 29678	http://www.thebooksmith.com
The Wild Burro Bookstore 503 North River Street Hot Springs, SD 57747	http://www.thewildburro.com
Little Professor Book Center 3315 6th Ave. SE Aberdeen, SD 57401	http://www.littleprofessorsd.com

Rock Point Books 401 Broad Street Chattanooga, TN 37402	http://www.rockpointbooks.com
Davis-Kidd Booksellers 2121 Green Hills Village Dr. Nashville, TN 37215	http://www.daviskidd.com
Blue Willow Bookshop 14532 Memorial Drive Houston, TX 77079	http://www.bluewillowbookshop.com
Kathy Budget Books 2450 Fry Rd. Houston, Texas 77084	http://www.katybooks.com
Sam Weller's Zion Bookstore 254 South Main Street Salt Lake City, UT 84101	http://www.samwellers.com
Golden Braid Books 151 South 500 East Salt Lake City, Utah 84102	http://www.goldenbraidbooks.com
Village Square Booksellers 32 the Square Bellows Falls, VT 05101	http://www.villagesquarebooks.com
The Norwich Bookstore Post Office Box 307 Norwich, VT 05055	http://www.norwichbookstore.com
Little Dickens and Givens Books 2236 Lakeside Dr. Lynchburg, VA 24501	http://www.givensbooks.com
Prince Books 109 E. Main Street Norfolk, VA 23510	http://www.prince-books.com
Square One Books 4724 - 42nd Avenue SW Seattle, WA 98116-4552	http://www.square1books.com
Garfield Book Co. at PLU 208 Garfield Street, Suite 101 Tacoma,WA,98444	http://luteworld.plu.edu
Taylor Books 226 Capitol St. Charleston, WV 25301	http://www.taylorbooks.com

Four Seasons Books 116 W. German St. P.O. Box 70 Shepherdstown, WV 25443	http://www.fourseasonsbooks.com/N ASApp/store/IndexJsp
20th Century Books 1421 S. Park Street, Suite 200 Madison WI 53715	http://www.southparkbooks.com
Rainbow Bookstore Co- operative 426 W. Gilman Street Madison, WI 53703	http://www.rainbowbookstore.org
Blue Heron Books & Espresso Atrium Plaza 201 East Second Street Casper, WY 82601	http://www.blueheronwyoming.com/s tore/index.php
Sheridan Stationery 206 North Main Street Sheridan, WY 82801	http://www.sheridanstationery.com

APPENDIX E

BLACK OWNED BOOKSTORES

(You can buy this mailing list at:

http://sbzshop.corecommerce.com/MAILING-LIST/)

Black Classics - Books and Gifts 140-B S. Sage Ave Mobile, AL 36606
Paradise Books 9008 N. 99th Street, suite 6 Peoria, AZ 85345-6948
Africa Enterprises 707 E. Broadway W. Memphis, AR 72301
Pyramid Art Books 500 President Clinton Avenue, suite 110 Little Rock, AR 72201
African Heritage Books and Gifts 5191 3rd Street San Francisco, CA 94124
The African Book Mart 2440 Durant Ave Berkeley, CA 94704-1611
Books In Color 5444 Watt Ave. Suite 900B North Highlands, CA 95660
Bright Lights Bookstore Attn: Michael McAllen 8461 S. Van Ness Ave. Inglewood, CA 90305
Black Spring Books Attn: Jerry Thompson 503 Georgia Street Vallejo, CA 94589

Eso Won Books
4331 Degnan Blvd.
Los Angeles, CA 90008

Hanna's Ethnic Bookseller
Attn: Carter A. Hanna
240 Blue Mountain Way
Claremont, CA 91711-2825

IronWood Corner
462 Toolen Place
Pasadena, CA 91103

Kongo Square Gallery
4334 Degnan Blvd.
Los Angeles, CA 90008

Marcus Books
1714 Filmore Ave.
San Francisco, CA 94115-3130

Phenix Information Center
381 N. E Street
San Bernardino, CA 92401

The Mecca of Information
20220 S. Avalon Blvd. Suite D
Carson, CA 90746

Zahra's Books and Things
900 North La Brea Ave.
Inglewood, CA 90302

Underground Books
2814 35th Street
Sacramento, CA 95817

Black and Read
7821 Wadsworth Blvd.
Arvada, CO 80003-2107

Black Books Galore Inc.
65 High Ridge Road, #407
Stamford, CT 06905-3806

Blackprint Heritage Gallery
162 Edgewood Ave.
New Haven, CT 06511-4522

Dygnyti Books
828 Dixwell Avenue
Hamden, CT 06514

EDEN Books
680 Blue Hills Avenue
Hartford, CT 06112

African-American Heritage Books
515 1/2 Northwood Rd. West
West Palm Beach, FL 33407-5817

African Book Store
3600 W. Broward Blvd.
Fort Lauderdale, FL 33312-1014

Books For Thought, Inc.
10910 N. 56th Street
Terrace Village Plaza
Tampa, FL 33617

Ethnic Elegance
9501 Arlington Expwy
Jacksonville, FL 32225

Heritage Bookstore and More
2219 Fowler Ave.
Fort Myers, FL 33901

Irmine's Books
PO Box 245342
Pembroke Pines, FL 33024

Montsho BookFairs, Etc., Inc.
2009 W. Central Blvd.
Orlando, FL 32805

Nefertiti Books
3574 Chappi Way
Jacksonville, FL 32223

Pyramid Books
544-2 Gateway Blvd.
Boynton Beach, FL 33435

Tenaj Books and Gift Gallery
608 5. US 1
Fort Pierce, FL 34954

Oasis Books
South Dekalb Mall
2801 Candler Rd
Decatur, GA 30034

Celebrate
1015 Patina Pt.
Peachtree City, GA 30269-4013

The Crowning Seat of Wisdom, Inc.
1130 Jackson St.
Madison, GA 30650

Medu Bookstore
2841 Greenbriar Parkway SW
Atlanta, GA 30331

Nubian Bookstore
2449 Southlake Mall
Morrow, GA 30260

The Reading Room Bookstore
56 Marietta St. NW
Atlanta, GA 30303

Shrine of the Black Madonna Bookstore
946 R.D. Abernathy Blvd. SW
Atlanta, GA 30310

The Tree of Life Bookstore of Harlem
1701 M.L. King Drive SW
Atlanta, GA 30314-2227

Two Friends Bookstore
598 Cascade Rd.
Atlanta, GA 30310

African-American Images Inc.
P.O. Box 1799
Sauk Village, IL 60412

Afri-Ware
226 West Lake St.
Oak Park, IL 60302

Afrocentric Book Store
4655 South King Drive.
Chicago, IL 60653

The Underground Bookstore
1727 E 87th St
Chicago, IL 60617

Frontline Dist Intl Inc.
5206 South Harper Ave
Chicago, IL 60615

Creative Hands Books
280 East Commercial St.
Pulaski, IL 62976

Free Your Mind
601 Roosevelt Road
Maywood, IL 60153-3237

Heritage Books
1135 West Granville Ave.
Chicago, IL 60660-2012

Knowledge Center Books
7001-a State Street
East Saint Louis, IL 62203-1331

X-Pression
5912 N. College Ave.
Indianapolis, IN 46220-2554

Afro-American Book Shop
7166 Crowder Blvd., Suite 103
New Orleans, LA 70127

Community Book Center
2523 Bayou Road
New Orleans, LA 70119

African American Books and Publishing
5116 Liberty Heights Ave.
Baltimore, MD 21207

Afrikan World Books
2217 Pennsylvania Ave.
Baltimore, Maryland 21217

Ascension Books
5490 Cedar Lane
suite B3
Columbia, MD 21044

Black By Popular Deman 5711 Ager Rd. Hyattsville, MD 20782-2602
Everyone's Place African Cultural Center 1380 W. North Ave. Baltimore, MD 21217
Karibu Bookstore 2103 Brightseat Rd. Landover, MD 20784
MasterWorks Books 2703 Curry Drive Adelphi, MD 20783
Sepia, Sand & Sable 6796 Reistersttown Rd. Baltimore, MD 21215
Reality Speaks Bookstore and Media Center 219 E. 25th Street Baltimore, MD 21218
Vertigo Books 7346 Baltimore Avenue College Park, MD 20740-3206
The Black Library 325 Huntington Ave., suite 83 Boston, MA 02115
Black Orchid Books 105 Columbia St. Maiden, MA 02148-3017
Apple Book Center 7900 W. Outer Drive Detroit, MI 48235
Forewords Books & Gifts Located in Originations Gallery 1671 Plymouth Rd. Ann Arbor, MI 48105 734-662-9197

Mahogany Books
15768 Biltmore
Detroit, MI 48227-1558

Shrine of the Black Madonna
Book Store and Cultural Center
13535 Livernois Ave.
Detroit, MI 48238

The Truth Bookstore
Northland Mall #476
21500 Northwestern Highway
Southfield, MI 48075

Uhuru Books
2917 Lyndale Ave. S
Minneapolis, MN 55407

Afro World
7676 Natural Bridge Rd.
Saint Louis, MO 63121-4905

Cultural Essentials
2127 S. Jefferson St.
Saint Louis, MO 63104-2209

First World657
North West Plaza
Saint Ann, MO 63074-2204

Left Bank Books
399 North Euclid
Saint Louis, MO 63108-1245

Treasures of the Mind Bookstore
6277 Delmar (in the University City Loop)
St. Louis, MO 63130

Ujamaa Maktaba UNLIMITED
4267 Manchester.
St. Louis, MO 63110-3850

Adhiambo Bookstore
3424 Robinson St.
Jackson, MS 39209-6731

Heritage Center
200 Sandy Lane
Vicksburg, MS 39183-9407

Shabaka's ??
3505 Tembaton Square Blvd
Vicksburg, MS 39180

Too-No Books Etc.
PO Box 8203
Moss Point, MS 39562

Aframerica Book Store
3226 Lake Street
Omaha, NE 68111

African American Book Store
216 1st St.
Hackensack, NJ 07601-2400

Books 'n Things
Cross Keys Plaza
3501 Rte 42
Turnersville, NJ 08080

Horizons Bookstore
171-169 B Market Street
Newark, NJ 07102

Kujichagulia Book Store
150-154 Ellison Street
Paterson, NJ 07505

Mind & Soul Bookstore, Inc.
449 S. Broad St.
Trenton, NJ 08611

Netu Khisa Books and Gifts
131-133 South Orange Avenue
South Orange, NJ 07079

Our Story Bookstore
1318 South Avenue
Plainfield, NJ 07062

Righteous Mind Books
39 N. Hermitage Ave.
Trenton, NJ 08618

Sacred Thoughts Bookstore
30 Mall Drive West
Jersey City, NJ 07310

Serengeti Plains
615 Bloomfield Ave.
Montclair, NJ 07042

Tunde Dada House of Africa
356 Main Street
Orange, NJ 07050

Aframerica Book Store
163 Mamaroneck Ave.
White Plains, NY 10601

Brownstone Books
409 Lewis Avenue
Brooklyn, NY 11233

A&B Books
1000 Atlantic Ave.
Brooklyn, NY 11238

Hue-Man Bookstore & Cafe
2319 Frederick Douglass Blvd
Between 124th and 125th Streets
New York, NY 10027

The Schomburg Center for Research into Black Culture
515 Malcolm X Blvd.
New York, NY 10037-1801

The Studio Museum of Harlem
144 West 125th St.
New York, NY 10027

BlackBookPlus.com
PO Box 030064
Elmont, NY 11003

Blacknificent Books & More
2011 Poole Rd.
Raleigh, NC 27610

Special Occasions Bookstore
112 North Martin Luther King Jr. Drive
Winston-Salem, NC 27101

The Know Bookstore
2520 Fayetteville St.
Durham, NC 27707

A Cultural Exchange
12621 Larchmere Blvd.
Cleveland, OH 44120-1109

Brighter Day Books & Gifts
5941 Hamilton Ave.
Cincinnati, OH 45224-3045

Timbuktu
5508 Superior Ave.
Cleveland, OH 44103

Reflections Coffee and Bookstore
Walnut Park Retail Center
446 NE Killingsworth St.
Portland, OR 97211

Afro-American Museum Bookstore
Seventh and Arch Streets
Philadelphia, PA 19106

Basic Black Books
Gallery One-Mall Level
9th & Market St.
Philadelphia, PA 19107

Gene's Books
PO Box 2517
Southeastern, PA 19399-2517

Know Thyself Bookstore and Cultural Development Center
528 S. 52nd St.
Philadelphia, PA 19143

Ligorius Bookstore Inc.
Cheltenham Square Mall Shopping Center
Philadelphia, PA 19150

Robbin's Bookstore
108 S. 13th Street
Philadelphia, PA 19107

Dorothea's African-American Books and Gifts
5410-D Two Notch Road
Columbia, SC 29204

Cokesbury Bookstore
2730 Broad River Rd.
Columbia, SC 29210

Alkebu-Lan Images Bookstore & Gift Shop
2721 Jefferson Street
Nashville, TN 37208

Book World
499 Merrit Ave.
Nashville, TN 37203

Black Images Book Bazaar
230 Wynnewood Village
Dallas, TX 75224

CushCity
13559 Bammel N. Houston Rd.
Houston, TX 77066

Babatunde & Yetunde
1102 W. Jaspter Rd.
Killeen, TX 76541

The Black Bookworm
605 E Berry St
Fort Worth, TX 76110-4300

Black Book Discounters
4720 La Branch
Houston, Texas 77004

Exhale African American Books & Gifts
5555 New Territory Blvd # 9102
Sugar Land, TX 77478

Jokae's African-American Books+
3917 W. Camp Wisdom
Suite #107
Dallas, TX 75237

MainStreet Books
4201 Main St
Houston, TX 77002

Nu World of Books
3250 Washington Blvd.
Beaumont, TX 77705

Out of Africa
Windsor Park Mall
7900 IH 35 N.
San Antonio, TX 78218

Shrine of the Black Madonna
5309 M.L.K. King
Houston, TX 77021

Tricia's Books N' Things
11975 Swords Creek
Houston, TX 77067

Sam Weller Books
254 S Main
Salt Lake City UT 84101

Atlantic Bookpost
PO Box 30552
Alexandria, VA 22310

One Force Books
217 E. Clay Street
Richmond, VA 23219

Positive Vibes
6220 B Indian River Rd.
Virginia Beach, VA. 23464

Words of Wisdom Books and Gifts
P.O. Box 4777
Norfolk, VA 23523

Brother\'s Books
11443 Rainier Ave. S.
Seattle, WA 98178-3954

Carol\'s Essentials Ethnic Gifts and Books
1106 23rd Avenue
Seattle, WA 98122

Howard University Bookstore
2225 Georgia Avenue, NW
Washington, DC 20059

Sankofa Video and Bookstore
2714 Georgia Ave., NW
Washington, DC 20001

The Sistrum (owned by Ausar Auset Society)
5920 Georgia Ave NW
Washington, DC 220011

Ujamaa Bookstore Afrikan Shop
1554 8th ST NW
Washington, DC 20001

Yawa Books
2206 18th St. NW
Washington, DC 20009-1813

The Cultural Connection Bookstore
3424 W. Villard Ave.
Milwaukee, WI 53209-4710

The Reader's Choice
1950 N. Dr. Martin Luther King Jr. Dr.
Milwaukee, WI 53212

APPENDIX F

AAFES DISTRIBUTORS

Tambra Estep The News Group / Mercury Retail Services (P.O. Box 18326) San Antonio, TX 78218 testep@mercretail.com	Lynn Crisp Doris Brookshire Great Atlantic News / The News Group 1955 Lakepark Dr., Ste. 400 Smyrna GA 30080 (770) 863-9019 lcrisp@thenewsgroup.com
Alison Roehr Chas Levy / Source Interlink 815 Ogden Ave Lisle, IL 60532 aroehr@sourceinterlink.com	Amber Hofseth Kent News 1402 Avenue B Scottsbluff NE 69361 (308) 635-2225 ahofseth@kentnews.com
Joe Murphy Harrisburg News 980 Briarsdale Road Harrisburg PA 17106-0307 (717) 561-8377 jmurphy@harrisburgnewsco.com www.harrisburgnewsco.com	Jim Kent Rushmore News 924 E. St Andrews St Rapid City SD 27701 (605) 342-2617 jkrushmore@rushmore.com
Clint Stiller The Hudson Group 1305 Paterson Plank Rd. North Bergen NJ 07047 (201) 867-3600 cstiller@hudsonnews.com	Steve Marcum Tri-County News 1376 W. Main Santa Maria, CA 93454-4999 (805) 925-6541 trico2000@aol.com
PMG International, Ltd. Attn: Mike Smith 1011 N. Frio (PO Box 7608) San Antonio TX 78207 (210) 212-3180 msmith@pmg-intl.com www.pmg-intl.com	Erik Sakariassen Saks News 2210 E. Broadway Bismark ND 58501 (701) 223-0818 ext 20 eriksaks@btinet.net

Rusty Schram Caribbean Management LLC 8167 N.W. 84th St. Medely, FL 33166 (305) 883-4420 rschram@carribeanmgmt.com	Julie Smith Benjamin News 1701 Rankin Missoula MT 59808 (703) 765-5626 juliesbng@qwestoffice.net
Bruce Bohach St. Marie's Gopher News Co. 9000 Tenth Ave. N. Minneapolis MN 55427-4344 (763) 546-5300 bab@gophernews.com	Steve Linville Great Pacific News / The News Group 1000 Oakesdale Ave., Suite 150 Renton WA 98057-1126 (425) 226-2023 slinville@thenewsgroup.com
Military Oriented Titles (Special Order vendor): Bill Donnis Byrrd Enterprises 1302 LaFayette Dr. Alexandria VA 22308 (703) 765-5626 byrrdbooks@aol.com	Mike Smith PMG International, Ltd. 1011 N. Frio (PO Box 7608) San Antonio TX 78207 (210) 212-3180 msmith@pmg-intl.com

APPENDIX G

EXAMPLES OF FLYERS/CATALOG
(FOR LIBRARIES/BOOKSTORES)

Example #1:

The Small Business Guide (U.S.) 2011 Edition
By Owen O. Daniels
owen@s-b-z.com

ABOUT THE AUTHOR:
A resident of Chicago, IL. A college graduate of John Jay College of Criminal Justice, with a Bachelor's degree in Public Administration (1985) and a graduate of Webster University with a Master in Computer Science (minor in Business Administration) 1989. The founder of two startup businesses.

The Small Business Guide

(U.S.)
2011 Edition

By Owen O. Daniels
The Small Business Zone, Inc.

Type: Paperback
Publication Date: 1 December 2010
ISBN: 9780982903612
Retail Price: $29.95

Distributors: Ingram Book Company & Baker & Taylor

CONTENTS

Now Millions of people who contemplate starting new small Businesses each year have a useful resource that they can turn to for information.

This is the book that people say they wish they had when they contemplated starting their business.

This is a practical and informative guide that provides actionable and timely information. No other book on this Subject provides the reader with this kind of information

Over 10 million people contemplate starting new businesses each year

Publisher: The Small Business Zone, Inc.
Publisher website: www.s-b-z.com
Intended Audience: Current and future
Entrepreneurs of all ages
Total pages: 204

Example #2:

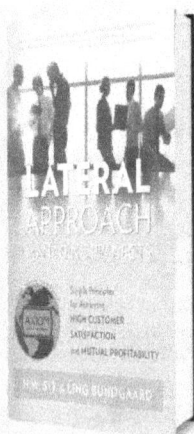

Example #3:

New Editions! Update your collection from Nova Publishing

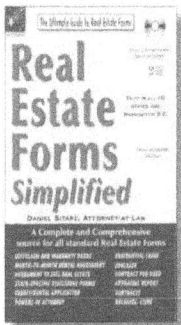

Real Estate Forms Simplified 2nd Edition

This revised and updated 2nd Edition includes all of the standard real estate forms that are needed for most common real estate transactions. Whether buying, selling, or leasing real estate, over one hundred valuable forms are included in this reference and as fillable PDF and text forms on the accompanying CD. The first edition was praised by American Reference Books Annual as "another superb volume in Nova's Business Made Simple Series...an exceptional value."

February, 2010~pb w/CD~256 pages~$29.95~7" x 9"~978-1-892949-49-3

Small Business Accounting Simplified 5th Edition

One of the most highly-acclaimed guides to business accounting and bookkeeping has now been revised and updated. This valuable reference now contains a CD with all forms as fillable PDF files. Written in plain and understandable language, with easy-to-use forms, this guide also includes the latest tax forms and instructions. Previous edition recommended by the Wall Street Journal online as "one of the best references for getting your finances in order."

February, 2010~pb w/CD~272 pages~$29.95~7" x 9"~978-1-892949-50-9

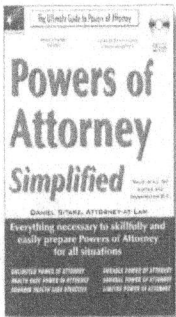

Powers of Attorney Simplified 2nd Edition

Powers of Attorney are valuable and useful legal forms that authorize another person to act on one's behalf. They may be used in business, legal, financial and health care situations. This comprehensive guide to the use of powers of attorney provides legal forms for all of the various situations in which powers of attorney may be employed. Unlimited, limited, general, durable, financial, and health care powers of attorney are included, as well as revocation forms. Dozens of state-specific forms are also provided. All of the forms are included on the enclosed CD in both fillable PDF and text file formats. The legal forms in this valuable reference are valid in all 50 states and Washington D.C.

Sept, 2010~pb w/CD~320 pages~$29.95~7" x 9"~978-1-892949-56-1

See other side for more titles

~ Ordering Information ~
National Book Network, 4501 Forbes Blvd. Ste. 200, Lanham, MD 20706
Phone orders (800)462-6420 Fax orders (800)338-4550

APPENDIX H

EXAMPLES OF FLYERS/CATALOG
(FOR DISTRIUTORS)

The Small Business Guide (U.S.) 2011 Edition
By Owen O. Daniels
owen@s-b-z.com

ABOUT THE AUTHOR:
A resident of Chicago, IL. A college graduate of John Jay College of Criminal Justice, with a Bachelor's degree in Public Administration (1985) and a graduate of Webster University with a Master in Computer Science (minor in Business Administration) 1989. The founder of two startup businesses.

The Small Business Guide

(U.S.)
2011 Edition

By Owen O. Daniels
The Small Business Zone, Inc.

CONTENTS

Type: Paperback
Publication Date: 1 December 2010
ISBN: 9780982903612
Retail Price: $29.95

WHOLESALE: Contact Createspace.com
 # per box (10.5" x 8.5" x 14.75"): 30
Reviews: Please visit our website and click on the review link

Now Millions of people who contemplate starting new small Businesses each year have a useful resource that they can turn to for information.

This is the book that people say they wish they had when they contemplated starting their business.

This is a practical and informative guide that provides actionable and timely information. No other book on this subject provides the reader with this kind of information.

Publisher: The Small Business Zone, Inc.
Publisher website: www.s-b-z.com
Intended Audience: Current and future
Entrepreneurs of all ages
Total pages: 204

INDEX

www.ingramcontent.com/pod-product-compliance
Lightning Source LLC
Chambersburg PA
CBHW072202270326
41930CB00011B/2510